SHORT CUTS

INTRODUCTIONS TO FILM STUDIES

FILM NOIR

FROM BERLIN TO SIN CITY

MARK BOULD

WALLFLOWER

LONDON and NEW YORK

A Wallflower Paperback

First published in Great Britain in 2005 by
Wallflower Press
6a Middleton Place, Langham Street, London W1W 7TE
www.wallflowerpress.co.uk

A catalogue record for this book is available from the British Library

ISBN 1 904764 50 9

Book design by Rob Bowden Design

Printed in Great Britain by Antony Rowe Ltd, Chippenham, Wiltshire

CONTENTS

ACKNOWLEDGEMENTS

It started out as a kind of joke, and then it wasn't funny any more because money became involved. Deep down, nothing about money is funny.
— Charles Willeford (2000: 3)

With thanks to Susan Alexander, Caroline Bainbridge, Emma Bircham, Anita Biressi, Andrew M. Butler, Istvan Csicsery-Ronay, Jr., Graham Fraser, Carl Freedman, Gillian Glitre, Joan Gordon, Veronica Hollinger, Rob Latham, Iris Luppa, China Miéville, Heather Nunn, Mike Sanders, Greg Tuck, friends and colleagues at BCUC and the journal *Historical Materialism*, my family and, above all, Kathrina Glitre — their friendship, solicitude and kindnesses made the year before I wrote this book easier to bear. Additional thanks to Iris for helpful comments on Weimar cinema; Carl for his Walter Neff secret; Mike Harrison for 'Fat Michael Douglas, every woman's dream'; and Kathrina for making this a better book than it would otherwise have been. Thanks also, of course, to Glenn Ford, Gloria Grahame, Ida Lupino, Robert Mitchum, Dick Powell, Robert Ryan, Barbara Stanwyck, Claire Trevor, Richard Widmark...

A NOTE ON TERMINOLOGY

Determinism argues that the state of a system at one moment gives rise to the state of that system in the following moment. Determinism should not be confused with fate, fatalism, cause-and-effect or predictability. Fate intrudes a metaphysics in which the entire history of a system, from which it is impossible to deviate, is laid down in advance. Fatalism is a resigned belief in this inescapable fate. Cause-and-effect is a narrative technique by which we make sense of the transition of a system from moment to moment. It is always a retrospective and partial account, an abstraction which marginalises or ignores the totality of the system. (It is, nonetheless, a useful tool for modelling the world and for telling it.) Predictability is the inverse of cause-and-effect. The ability to construct retrospective cause-and-effect chains implies that it should be possible to extend their construction into the future; this is an error based on forgetting that cause-and-effect is a retrospective abstraction. A determinist system does not require fate, inevitability, predictability or cause-and-effect. In the non-linear dynamics of complex systems, there is no necessary correspondence of magnitude between a microscopic fluctuation in a system and the macroscopic divergences it can produce in that system. This is not about a small cause having a large effect, but about the initial conditions of the entire system producing unforeseeable conditions in the system at a subsequent moment; it is about a sensitive dependence on initial conditions; it is about determinism without predictability. In complex systems, order can emerge from chaos, and chaos often contains deeply-encoded structures of order. (See Earman 1986, Hall 1992, Hayles 1990 and 1991, and Hoefer 2003.)

   The point of all this will become clear.

ON DANGEROUS GROUND: INTRODUCING FILM NOIR

One day in 1993, Emmy Award-winning filmmaker Ara Chekmayan visited a Pennsylvania fleamarket, where he discovered a statuette that looked exactly like the Maltese Falcon. Chekmayan purchased the black bird for $8 and, not long afterward, believing it to be one of two identical props that had been used in the famous 1941 Warner Bros. movie, he offered it up for auction at Christie's, who estimated its value at $50,000. Before an auction could take place, however, a Los Angeles collector pointed out that identical copies of the statuette could be purchased at $45 a piece from a book dealer in Long Beach...
    – James Naremore (1998: 254)

James Naremore takes this anecdote to prove that certain 1940s Hollywood thrillers have accumulated sufficient 'artistic and cultural cachet' to become 'valuable as other things besides movies' (1998: 255). Looked at differently, it provides a key to the central problematic of identifying, delineating, defining film noir: this book opens by quoting from another book on film noir which retells a story from *People* magazine about a man who found one of many copies based on the original (two copies of the) prop of the Maltese Falcon – which, diegetically, was a fake – in the third film to be based on Dashiell Hammett's 1931 hard-boiled detective novel *The Maltese Falcon*, itself originally serialised in *Black Mask* pulp magazine between September 1929 and January 1930. So what exactly was it that Chekmayan thought he had found when he thought he had found (one of) the original Falcon(s)? In this welter of copies of copies in different media and adaptations from one medium to another the notion of an original evanesces. Even Hammett is no guarantor. His cynical deflation of the Grail myth in the modern urban waste land is not the first (his 1931 *The Glass Key* alludes to T. S. Eliot's 1922 'The Waste Land'), nor is his Sam Spade the original hard-boiled detective (a more likely contender is Carroll John Daly's Terry Mack).

Similarly, when we approach film noir, we are faced with neither an objectively-existing object out there in the world nor some ideal to which particular films more or less conform. Instead, as Naremore argues, film noir 'has less to do with a group of artefacts than with a discourse – a loose evolving system of arguments and readings that helps to shape commercial strategies and aesthetic ideologies' (1998: 11). Like any genre, film noir is an intersubjective discursive phenomenon: a fabrication. But as Dudley Andrew observes, 'A fabrication ... is by no means a fiction' (1995: 12).

After indicating the number of films that have been considered film noirs, this introduction suggests how that canon might be further expanded and considers one influential attempt to more rigidly delineate the genre, detailing some of the difficulties implicit in it. Marc Vernet notes that 'the Americans made [film noir] and then the French invented it' (1993: 1). Chapter one therefore surveys some of the Francophone criticism which first identified – or fabricated the idea of – film noir before outlining some of the early Anglophone statements about film noir, showing how the idea was taken up and developed prior to the academicisation of film studies in the 1970s. The purpose of this chapter is to demonstrate the historically-contingent discursive fabrication of the genre.

If the idea of film noir originated in mid-1940s Paris, the origins of the genre are typically traced back to four sources: German expressionism, French poetic realism, American hard-boiled fiction and American crime films (see Richardson 1992 on Italian neorealism as a neglected influence). Chapter two expands the consideration of interwar German cinema beyond expressionism, noting similarities with Hollywood's 1930s fallen-women cycle before turning to the work of Robert Siodmak and Fritz Lang, German directors who made numerous film noirs in exile. It then considers 1930s French cinema, contrasting several poetic realist films with American film noirs. It examines 1930s American crime films, particularly the gangster cycle – how the anachronistic figure of the 1930s gangster proved integral to the meaning of 1940s film noirs, and how the moratorium on producing gangster pictures produced alternative kinds of crime film – and three films, two of them directed by Lang, in which the increasing psychologisation of crime already apparent in hard-boiled fiction can be traced. In focusing on these filmic sources, the treatment of literary sources will remain cursory (on hard-boiled fiction, see Forter 2000, Madden 1968, Marling 1995, McCann 2000, Nolan 1985, O'Brien 1997, O'Connell 2002).

Chapter three offers detailed consideration of a variety of film noirs from the main cycle, which began with *Stranger on the Third Floor* (1940) and *The Maltese Falcon* (1941). Production peaked in the late 1940s and early 1950s and continued into the late 1950s, petering out with *Cape Fear* (1962), *The Manchurian Candidate* (1962), *Shock Corridor* (1963) and *The Naked Kiss* (1964). The films treated in this chapter were selected in order to explore the genre's recurring concern with notions of determinism, particularly the constitution and shaping – and simultaneous shattering and dissolution – of individual subjectivity. By examining two overlapping groups of film noirs – one dominated by images and ideas of entrapment, the other by images and ideas of investigation – this chapter does not argue that these are the primary concerns of the genre or even necessarily of these particular films, but rather explores how they are articulated in a significant proportion of film noirs. The construction of gender, particularly white masculinities, is a recurring concern throughout (on film noir and race, see Diawara 1993, Kaplan 1998b, Oliver and Trigo 2003).

Chapter four offers a brief overview of the development of neo-noir, culminating in a discussion of *Femme Fatale* (2002), a film whose self-conscious combination of various elements of film noir, spectacle-dominated action movie and erotic thriller is typical of many neo-noirs (as are its homophobia, misogyny and racism), while its major plot twist combines a fantastic coincidence which rearticulates noirish determinism.

Finally, the afterword considers *This Is Not a Love Song* (2002) and *Sin City* (2005) as digital remediations of film noir.

The inclusive filmography offered by Paul Duncan (2003) lists 1,028 film noirs:

German expressionist films, 1920–33	5
American precursors, 1927–39	26
French poetic realist films, 1931–43	8

American film noirs, 1940–60	647
American noir westerns, 1940–53	7
American post-noirs, 1961–76	48
American neo-noirs, 1976–92	167
French films, 1949–91	31
British films, 1927–91	71
Italian films, 1943–71	5
Mexican films, 1949–71	3
Japanese films, 1962–2000	10

Foster Hirsch (1999) lists a further 47 American neo-noirs released between 1993 and 1997, and Robin Buss (1994) a further 79 French film noirs between 1942 and 1992. Although Andrew Spicer (2002) only lists 538 films, this includes almost 200 titles not mentioned by these other authors, many of them among the 104 British film noirs he identifies. These figures illustrate two important points.

First, that the main cycle of American film noirs is recorded in sufficient detail that, despite the debatable inclusion of many of the titles in these encyclopaedic listings, few more additions are likely to be unearthed, although some might arise from critically rethinking other genres, especially melodrama and, possibly, the western. Several westerns – *Pursued* (1947), *Ramrod* (1947), *High Noon* (1952), *Rancho Notorious* (1952), the five James Stewart westerns directed by Anthony Mann – have been described as noir westerns and many more from the 1950s feature badly disturbed protagonists or, like some scenes in *My Darling Clementine* (1946), noirish lighting. Additionally, several film noirs utilise western imagery: Florian's bar in *Murder, My Sweet* (1944) seems to be an only-slightly-redressed western saloon, complete with swinging doors and music that stops when Marlowe (Dick Powell) and Moose Malloy (Mike Mazurki) enter; in *High Sierra* (1941) and *White Heat* (1949) western costumes and settings anachronise their protagonists; in *Gun Crazy* (1950) similar costumes expose the tendency to romanticise crime and outlaws even as, contradictorily, it depicts a passionate *amour fou*. Furthermore, the growing number of science fiction films which play on and with film noir conventions, from *Alphaville* (1965) to *Cypher* (2003), might encourage a re-examination of earlier science fiction films for traces of or affiliations to film noir.

Second, that outside of the main period of American film noir the terrain is still lacking any kind of consensus. There is still work to be done on film noirs before film noir, film noirs after film noir and film noirs in other national, linguistic and international contexts. For example, Michael Walker suggests that further research into 1930s crime films might produce 'more proto-*noir* films' (1992a: 33) like *Nancy Steele is Missing* (1936), and James Naremore notes the critical neglect of the direct-to-video industry – in the mid-1990s, a 'seventeen-billion-dollar-a-year industry, involving more money than all the major studios combined' (1998: 161) – which produces numerous softcore erotic thrillers, perhaps the primary contemporary manifestation of film noirs about sexual obsession, blackmail and murder. Similarly, research into other national cinemas might uncover more films like the Japanese *Keisatsukan* (1933), while discussions of neo-noir have yet to consider East Asian crime cinema in detail. Furthermore, if one accepts that film noirs are still being made, then each fresh example could potentially reshape the genre, narrowing or, more probably, widening it. Questions of omissions and additions inevitably return to questions of definition, and any attempt at definition restructures the genre, drawing in or casting out particular titles. It is through such complex feedback processes that genres form and reform.

In 1978, James Damico proposed a working model of film noir in terms of characters and plot structure so as to cut through the ill-discipline of encyclopaedic listings and the confusions they engender:

> Either because he is fated to do so by chance, or because he has been hired for a job specifically associated with her, a man whose experience of life has left him sanguine and often bitter meets a not-innocent woman of similar outlook to whom he is sexually and fatally attracted. Through this attraction, either because the woman induces him to it or because it is the natural result of their relationship, the man comes to cheat, attempt to murder, or actually murder a second man to whom the woman is unhappily or unwillingly attached (generally he is her husband or lover), an act which often leads to the woman's betrayal of the protagonist, but which in any event brings about the sometimes metaphoric, but usually literal destruction of the woman, the man to whom she is attached, and frequently the protagonist himself. (1996: 137)

This narrative structure, familiar from James M. Cain's novels *The Postman Always Rings Twice* (1934) and *Double Indemnity* (1936), is found in the nine films, uncontroversially film noirs, on which Damico focuses: *Double Indemnity* (1944), *The Woman in the Window* (1945), *Scarlet Street* (1945), *The Killers* (1946), *The Postman Always Rings Twice* (1946), *Out of the Past* (1947), *The Lady from Shanghai* (1948), *Pitfall* (1948) and *Criss Cross* (1949). Damico suggests that *Murder, My Sweet* (1944), *The Strange Love of Martha Ivers* (1946) and *The Blue Dahlia* (1946) contain only 'slight variations', while *The Maltese Falcon* anticipates key aspects and *In a Lonely Place* (1950) contains 'apparent mutations and [a] collapsing of elements' (1996: 138).

Although Damico recognises that there are 'a multitude of other correspondences to be evaluated which will perhaps delimit, broaden or even invalidate this provisional model', including 'the pervasive atmosphere of corruption, crime, psychopathology and evil; the constant resort to gratuitous violence; the omnipresence of the returning veteran; the importance of the oneiric in structure and substance; and recurrent visuals' (ibid.), he argues that it can be used to exclude certain films from the film noir canon, such as the postwar semi-documentary films which reconstructed actual crimes, pioneered by producer Louis de Rochemont and beginning with *The House on 92nd Street* (1945). Damico also claims that his model enables an understanding of how, in other films, the 'elements have been altered and condensed or expanded' (1996: 139), but his example of giggling psychopath Tommy Udo (Richard Widmark) in *Kiss of Death* (1947) as someone who combines 'the masculine and feminine qualities of the other man and the fatal woman' (ibid.) conveniently overlooks the film's indebtedness to the semi-documentary cycle.

Damico's elaborations demonstrate a tension in any attempt to delimit a genre, best understood through the distinction between semantic and syntactic approaches to genre. Semantic approaches catalogue 'common traits, attitudes, characters, shots, locations' (Altman 1999: 219), and then list all the films which contain (at least some of) them. Despite generating exhaustive lists, this approach has little explanatory power. In contrast, syntactic approaches like Damico's model identify and explore 'certain constitutive relationships between undesignated and variable place-holders' (ibid.) in a handful of canonical texts seen as exemplifying the particular genre's core concerns. However, no sooner than Damico imposes a syntactic model he expands his initially exclusive list into a far more inclusive one, reinterpreting and reshaping excluded films so that they more closely approximate to his model and can therefore be readmitted into the genre. Indeed, this problem is evident even in the nine films he considers an unequivocal match for his model, as a description of *The Killers* will show.

Two hitmen, Al (Charles McGraw) and Max (William Conrad), arrive in Brentwood, New Jersey, take over Henry's Diner and await the arrival of Swede (Burt Lancaster), who works at the gas station. When he fails to appear, the hitmen head for his boarding house. Warned of their approach, Swede, who has clearly been waiting for something like this to happen, refuses to do anything, explaining, 'I did something wrong – once'. He is killed. This opening sequence, a textbook example of film noir lighting and composition, is based on Ernest Hemingway's story 'The Killers' (1928), which ends at this point. The remainder of the film takes the form of a quest to uncover the reason for Swede's murder. Insurance investigator Riordan (Edmond O'Brien) is intrigued. In the first of the film's eleven flashbacks, he learns that a stranger – Colfax (Albert Dekker) – stopped for gas several days earlier, since when Swede had been laid up in his room, 'sick'. Riordan traces Swede's beneficiary, Queenie (Queenie Smith), a maid at an Atlantic City hotel where Swede stayed with a woman for several days in 1940, who recalls Swede's attempted suicide after the woman left him. Swede's former boxing career leads Riordan to Lieutenant Sam Lubinsky (Sam Levene), Swede's childhood friend who became a cop. Sam's first flashback is to the night of Swede's last fight, when he injured his hand so badly he had to quit boxing. Sam's wife, Lilly (Virginia Christine), who used to be Swede's girlfriend, introduces a flashback in which it becomes clear that Swede then became involved with criminals, falling for Kitty Collins (Ava Gardner), the mistress of the incarcerated Colfax. In Sam's second flashback he tells of arresting Swede when he insisted on taking the rap for Kitty. At Swede's funeral, Riordan meets Charleston (Vince Barnett), Swede's ex-cellmate. In a pair of flashbacks, he tells Riordan about Swede's obsession with Kitty, and how he introduced Swede to Colfax; Charleston refused to become involved in the heist Colfax was planning, but Swede, lured by Kitty's presence, agreed. The eighth flashback is narrated by Riordan's boss, who reads a newspaper account of the 1940 Prentiss Hat Company robbery which Riordan has linked to Swede. Sam summons Riordan to a hospital where Blinky (Jeff Corey), one of Colfax's gang, is dying of gunshot wounds. Delirious, he introduces two flashbacks: in the first, on the eve of the robbery, Swede threatens Colfax; in the second, Swede, claiming that he has been double-crossed, arrives at the altered rendezvous after the robbery and takes all the money. Riordan returns to Swede's room in Brentwood where Dum-Dum (Jack Lambert), the gang member who killed Blinky, is searching for a clue as to where Swede hid the money. After a scuffle, Dum-Dum escapes. Riordan questions Colfax, now an apparently respectable businessman, who denies all knowledge of the robbery. Riordan arranges a meeting with Kitty. She introduces the final flashback, in which she convinces Swede the gang are double-cross-ing him so as to get him to double-cross them. It was, however, all a set-up, a complex double-cross planned by Colfax, to whom Kitty is now married. Back in the present, Sam kills the hitmen as they try to gun down Riordan, but Kitty escapes. Riordan, Sam and the police arrive at Colfax's house to find Dum-Dum dead and Colfax dying. Colfax, who stumbled across Swede, killed him so that no-one from the gang might find him and thus work out that Colfax and Kitty actually stole the money. Kitty arrives, but Colfax refuses to falsely clear her name before he dies.

This account demonstrates the extent of the violence Damico must perform on *The Killers* for it to conform to his model. If the film, shot by Woody Bredell, is a virtual inventory of film noir's low-key, expressionist cinematography, it is also a compendium of film noir plots. Walker sug-gests that it forms, along with *Criss Cross* and *The File on Thelma Jordan* (1950), Siodmak's trilogy 'dealing with "the mystery of woman"' (1992b: 151), and Damico's narrative structure *can* be found in the flashback story, albeit with deviations. Although Kitty does induce Swede to cheat Colfax, it is only as part of a larger scheme with Colfax, and there is little to suggest that Kitty is 'unhappily or unwillingly attached' to Colfax. This triangular relationship is simultaneously at the centre of the film and marginalised because the narrative foregrounds Riordan's investigation. Kitty's femme fatale and Swede's victim-hero, character types at the centre of Damico's model, are subordinated and subjected to Riordan's seeker-hero narrative (on these character types, see Walker 1992a). The film might then be better understood as a male investigation of the mystery of a man, lending it a homoerotic frisson.

The film was initially perceived as a gangster film – Siodmak retrospec-tively regarded it as such – and Walker suggests that it can be also seen, with *Criss Cross* and *Cry of the City* (1948), as part of Siodmak's gangster trilogy (1992b: 128). It is also, like *Body and Soul* (1947), *Champion* (1949), *The Set-Up* (1949), *Second Chance* (1953), *Killer's Kiss* (1955) and *The Harder They Fall* (1956), a boxing film noir. Swede's attempted double-cross is a shorthand form of the revenge against the mob plot which, despite appearing in film noirs like *The Big Heat* (1953) and *Underworld USA* (1961), did not come to fruition until *Point Blank* (1967) and *Get Carter* (1970). Swede and Kitty are briefly a couple on the run, like those in *They Live By Night* (1949) and *Gun Crazy*; and like *The Asphalt Jungle* (1950), *The Killing* (1956) and *Odds Against Tomorrow* (1959), *The Killers* also contains a heist. This robbery sequence, filmed in a single two-minute crane-shot, seems to belong in one of the semi-documentary crime films Damico wishes to exclude from the genre, an affiliation made stronger by the accompanying voice-over narration whose phrasing, tone, selection of detail and apparently objective omniscience resembles the semi-documentary's 'official account' voice. As these other elements suggest, Damico seriously reduces and misdescribes *The Killers* in order to cite it as exemplary of his model.

A further problem arises with this model when *The Killers* is compared to Don Siegel's 1964 remake. Two hitmen, Charlie (Lee Marvin) and Lee (Clu Gulager), track down Johnny North (John Cassavetes), an ex-racing driver who was involved in a million-dollar robbery some years earlier. Johnny's resignation puzzles the ageing Charlie, who wonders why he made no attempt to flee his killers, concluding that the only person who would pay to have him killed without trying to discover what happened to the stolen money would be the person who actually stole it. Hoping to retire, Charlie persuades Lee to help him track down whoever contracted the hit. They question Earl (Claude Akins), Johnny's old mechanic. In the film's first flashback, Earl tells how Johnny fell for Sheila Farr (Angie Dickinson), the mistress of gangster Jack Browning (Ronald Reagan). Johnny and Sheila plan to marry, but when a car crash leaves him unable to continue racing, he sends her away, believing he has been just another of her casual infidelities with physically active younger men. Charlie and Lee then track down Mickey Farmer (Norman Fell), an associate of Browning, who in flashback picks up the story: Sheila persuades Browning that they need a specialist driver for a heist he is planning and urges him to recruit Johnny; after the heist, Johnny stole the money from Browning and disappeared. When the hitmen trace Browning, he appears to be a legitimate businessman. They make him arrange a meeting with Sheila. She stonewalls them at first, but breaks down when they threaten to kill her. In the third flashback, narrated by Sheila, she convinces Johnny to rob Browning and run off with her. However, it was all part of a scheme for her and Browning to get the money and leave the rest of the gang thinking that Johnny had it. As they leave the hotel to retrieve the money, a sniper kills Lee and injures Charlie. Sheila escapes and Browning – the sniper – joins her at their house. As they empty the safe, Charlie, blood dripping from his wound, catches up with them. He kills Browning. When Sheila pleads for her life, Charlie replies, 'Lady, I don't have the time', and shoots her. He stumbles from the house with the money and collapses, dead.

From this description, the remake might seem considerably more noir-ish than the original. The investigation is conducted by a pair of professional killers rather than official or semi-official detectives, one world-weary and cold, the other narcissistic and brutal. They are motivated by curiosity, cash and, one suspects, a need to do something between contracts; and they both die. While Kitty remains an enigma primarily because she is largely absent from a film whose entire plot hinges on her manipulation of Swede, Sheila remains an enigma because, hidden behind mask-like makeup, she is the contradictory product of an experiment in perspectivism. In the first flashback, she seems genuinely to fall for Johnny, telling him she loves him and intends to stand by him after his accident. In the second flashback, the audience is manipulated into believing she has been searching for Johnny because she still has feelings for him. When she finds him, Browning spies on her through binoculars, and only after she offers to find Johnny some well-paid work does she set about persuading Browning to employ him. The first flashback contained scenes Earl did not witness but convention implies their objectivity, a sense reinforced by showing Sheila, whom Earl did not like, in a positive light (it is Johnny who rejects Sheila, not vice versa). Consequently, we are lured into accepting the apparent objectivity of the second flashback. It is only in the third flashback that we realise Mickey's account of the heist is actually an account of what he *thought* had happened; but to the extent that we accept it as objective while it unfolds, Sheila's betrayal of Johnny seems all the more devastating.

Siodmak's version contrasts the noir world with a more respectable existence exemplified by the Lubinskys' roof terrace, itself an extension of the contrast between the femme fatale Kitty and the domestic Lilly. This is ironised by the artifice of the rooftop idyll. The well-lit set is obviously a set and although it is above the noir world, it is a cramped space, confined by roof tops and chimney pots – but nonetheless it endures. After his final fight, Swede has the option of attaining this domestic idyll. Lilly was still his girlfriend and Sam offered to get him a job in the police with a steady income and a pension, but Swede sent Lilly home and parted company with Sam, turning down a noirishly-lit dark alley. (The more-than-passing facial resemblance between Swede and Riordan further emphasises this sense of alternative paths taken into alternative worlds.) Siegel's version, which was made for television but released in cinemas, offers no such contrast. It is brightly- and uniformly-lit, conventionally-shot and in colour. Killers kill with impunity and law-enforcement agents are completely absent, appearing only as the sound of approaching sirens at the end. Arguably, the noir world has become ubiquitous and normalised, rendering a stylistically distinct representation superfluous or impossible. However, because it rejects film noir's visual style, the consensus is that the remake, despite being closer to Damico's model, is the less noirish version. To the extent that this is a reasonable judgement, film noirs cannot be defined solely in terms of a narrative structure.

What Damico offers is a narrative formula which recurs in some form in a significant number of film noirs, but which cannot be regarded as exclusive to film noirs unless one is prepared to include all films that follow the formula in the genre and to exclude all those which do not. Hammett's *Red Harvest* (1929) and its film adaptations demonstrate the problems with this approach. The novel, featuring an unnamed detective, closely matches the narrative structure of the classic western, exemplified by *Shane* (1953), in which a 'lone stranger … rides into a troubled town and cleans it up' (Wright 1977: 32), but it has a contemporary setting and a jaded, cynical tone. Although there is no difficulty in counting one of its adaptations, *Per un pugno di dollari* (1964), as a western, the novel itself and the two other adaptations, the samurai film *Yojimbo* (1961) and the gangster film *Last Man Standing* (1996), are rather more problematic. Clearly there are ways in which they can be regarded as westerns, but in doing so one must recognise that genres are rather more fluid than Damico allows and that films have multiple generic tendencies.

In addition, then, to sharing several sometimes overlapping and interacting narrative (and thematic) structures, film noirs also share elements of a distinctive visual style. Low-key lighting and the positioning of key-, fill- and back-lighting produced patterns of light and dark which were, by Hollywood standards, unconventional. Increased depth of field made shots more ambiguous and, particularly during night-for-night shooting, required wide-angle lenses which also distorted foreground figures. Unbalanced and disharmonious compositions introduced tension into the *mise-en-scène*, subjectivising the objective third-person camera by shaping the diegesis to express the conflicts within and between characters. (On film noir style, see Bordwell, Staiger and Thompson 1988, Place and Peterson 1974; on industrial and economic determinants of this style, see Kerr 1996, Lev 2003, Maltby 2003, Schatz 1997.)

However, despite the importance of visual style to film noirs, the claim made by several critics that film noir is a style rather than a genre seems as untenable as the claims made for a specific narrative (or thematic) structure. Rather, film noirs emerge from (discussions about) the interactions of style, narrative and theme. Therefore, the solution this book adopts to the problem of defining film noir – it is, of course, no solution – is to avoid suggesting that a genre can be defined by a single paradigm. Rather it will explore the genre from several angles and attempt to represent as much of the narrative, thematic, stylistic and temporal range of film noir as possible.

1 THE SET-UP: FABRICATING FILM NOIR

Talk is dangerous. Sometimes it makes things happen, it makes them real.
  – *Body Heat* (1981)

Film noir, like the femme fatale, is an elusive phenomenon: a projection of desire, always just out of reach. The task of delineating and circumscribing film noir, of pinning it down, frequently recalls the convoluted constructions of identity around a central absence in *Vertigo* (1958). Scottie (James Stewart), who retired from the police because of his vertigo, is hired by Gavin Elster (Tom Helmore) to investigate his wife, Madeleine (Kim Novak). She is possessed, apparently, by the spirit of her grandmother, Carlotta, who was driven to despair and suicide. When his vertigo keeps him from preventing Madeleine's suicide, Scottie has a breakdown. A year later, he meets Judy Barton (Kim Novak), whom he attempts to reshape into the image of Madeleine. Unknown to him, Gavin had hired Judy to pretend to be Madeleine in order to enable him to murder the real Madeleine. This information is revealed to the audience as soon as Scottie meets Judy – he only realises the truth after he has recreated (the false) Madeleine – and completely alters one's understanding of what we have already seen.

About halfway through the film, the false-Madeleine wakes up in Scottie's apartment, having been rescued by him after her (fake) suicide attempt. As they talk for the first time, a mutual attraction is signalled: but to what are they attracted and with whom are they falling in love? Judy, pretending to be Madeleine (who has been possessed by Carlotta), falls for Scottie, who is pretending that he has not been hired by Gavin and following her around all day, while Judy, pretending to be Madeleine, is pretending not to know that Scottie has been hired by Gavin and following her around all day. Infinite regress threatens. Similarly, when Scottie reshapes Judy as Madeleine, of what does his model actually consist? Madeleine? Judy as Madeleine? Judy as her idea of Madeleine? Judy as Gavin's idea of Madeleine? It is fitting, then, that the film opens with vortices – vaginal images, elaborate structures around empty cores – and closes with Scottie, atop a phallic tower, confronting an abyss. Identity, *Vertigo* suggests, remains a mystery, an aporia around which can be found prosaic realities (Judy is from Selina, Kansas and can prove it) and elusive trails (Madeleine is an absence, seen only once, in flashback, already dead). Likewise, film noir.

It is customary to acknowledge that film noir was a retrospectively-applied generic label; consequently, no-one could ever have set out to make a film noir because the signifier (and thus what it signified) had not entered into English usage at the time the films now called film noirs were actually made. Suggestions that this might invalidate film noir's generic status tend to overlook the fact that the introduction and circulation of a generic label for a group of related texts *must* come after the creation of those texts, that generic labelling must always be, at least initially, retrospective. For example, Charles Musser situates *The Great Train Robbery* (1903) – the so-called first western – within the railway sub-genre of the then popular travel genre of films, arguing that director Edwin S. Porter 'was consciously working (and cinema patrons viewing) within a framework' derived from 'the violent crime genre which had been imported from England a few months earlier', and that because it was not 'primarily perceived in the context of the western' its success 'did not encourage other westerns but other films of crime' (1990: 130–1).

While Steve Neale is correct to be concerned about the homogenising effect of imposing film noir as a generic category, this is common to all applications of generic terminology. Similarly, although Neale's willingness to concede that 'film noir now has a generic status it originally did not possess' (2000: 3) seems to imply that this is unique to film noir, it is true of any genre: one cannot now stop seeing *The Great Train Robbery* as a western even though in 1903 the genre 'had not yet been established effectively in the cinema' (Musser 1990: 131) and even if one is aware of its other generic tendencies and affiliations. Genres arise – or, more accurately, are identified, named and developed – through complex feedback mechanisms involving producers, distributors, exhibitors, consumers, interpreters and other discursive agents. This chapter examines how film noir emerged as an intersubjective discursive phenomenon in French and Anglo-American criticism.

The term 'film noir' is said to derive from *Série noire*, the title of a series of crime novels edited by Marcel Duhamel for French publisher Gallimard, starting in 1945. Following translations of three novels by Peter Cheyney and James Hadley Chase (British writers imitating American models), the series began to translate novels by American writers like Raymond Chandler, Horace McCoy, Dashiell Hammett, W. R. Burnett, William P. McGivern, Cornell Woolrich, David Goodis and Chester Himes (from 1948, French authors were published under English pseudonyms and, after 1951, under their own names).

The term 'noir' was used in France before the Second World War, usually in the right-wing press to derogate left-wing culture (see O'Brien 1996), and some late 1930s films were described as 'film noirs' in the 1940s; but neither term was applied to American films until 1946. Following the liberation from German occupation, large numbers of American films were released in France. In 1946, Nino Frank linked *Double Indemnity*, *The Maltese Falcon*, *Murder, My Sweet* and *Laura* (1944) to the revolution in American crime fiction started by Hammett. Whereas previous fictional detectives, like C. Auguste Dupin, Philo Vance and Ellery Queen, were little more than perfectly functioning ratiocination devices, Hammett's Continental Op and Sam Spade, as well as Chandler's Philip Marlowe, were flawed characters. This difference, Frank argued, was manifest in the films' emphasis on character psychology rather than the investigation and retrospective reconstruction of particular crimes. In these film noirs, as he dubbed them, the crime film was psychologised by first-person narration and closely-observed facial expressions, gestures and dialogue.

Later that year, Jean-Pierre Chartier called *Double Indemnity*, *Murder, My Sweet*, *The Postman Always Rings Twice* and *The Lost Weekend* (1945) film noirs, suggesting they were so dark that French films like *Quai des brumes* (1938) and *Hôtel du nord* (1938) could no longer really be considered as film noirs. These pessimistic, misanthropic American films were driven by a logic of sexual desire that the Production Code Administration

(PCA) simultaneously required them to suppress. This pattern of desire and repression in the characters, matched by the filmmakers' double-coding, rendered the crime itself the object of the protagonists' erotic fascination, further psychologising the crime film. In 1948 Henri-François Rey, who regarded American cinema as propagandist, suggested that *Double Indemnity*, *The Lost Weekend*, *Scarlet Street* and *The Woman in the Window* presented views of the US so unflattering and despairing as to require special comment. In 1951, Pierre Duvillars considered the centrality of a new version of the vamp to *The Postman Always Rings Twice*, *Murder, My Sweet*, *Double Indemnity* and *Criss Cross*. A figure 'accommodated to contemporary taste, itself composed of cynicism, sadism and morbidness' (1996: 30), she reduces the male protagonist to a hypnotised, machine-like creature through the calculated but, he suggests, never consummated promise of sex. In their survey of American film noir originally published in 1955, Raymonde Borde and Etienne Chaumeton list 22 film noirs, from *The Maltese Falcon* to *Macao* (1951). A further 62 appear in related categories: 29 about criminal psychology and ten about social trends, seven costume crime films, six gangster films and ten documentary police thrillers. Except for the costume films, each category contains films now generally considered film noirs, whereas their list of film noirs includes *The Mask of Dimitrios* (1944), *Notorious* (1946), *Chicago Deadline* (1949) and *The Window* (1949), none of which are now deemed central to the genre.

James Naremore argues that the growing Americanism in postwar French culture and nostalgia for their pre-war cinema predisposed the French to discover or invent American film noir, and because of their affiliations with either surrealism or existentialism these early critics constructed it in particular ways. For surrealist aficionados like Borde and Chaumeton,

> the essence of noirness lies in a feeling of discontinuity, an intermingling of social realism and oneiricism, an anarcho-leftist critique of bourgeois ideology and an eroticised treatment of violence. Above all, noir produces a psychological and moral disorientation, an inversion of capitalist and puritan values, as if it were pushing the American system toward revolutionary destruction. We might debate whether such qualities are in fact essential to the Hollywood thriller ... but there is no question that they are fundamental to surrealist art. (Naremore 1998: 22)

For existentialist critics, film noirs 'depicted a world of obsessive return, dark corners or *huis-clos*' (ibid.). Where 'perversely anarchic' surrealists saw 'a theatre of cruelty', existentialists found a 'despairingly humanist' protoabsurdism (ibid.). This existentialist criticism can be traced through Jean-Paul Sartre to André Bazin, co-founder of *Cahiers du Cinéma*, a journal which carried essays by several critics who would go on to become New Wave filmmakers, including Claude Chabrol's 'Évolution du film policier' (1955). It was at this juncture that

> the terms *film noir* and *auteur* began to work in tandem, expressing the same values from different angles … Film noir was a collective style operating within and against the Hollywood system; and the auteur was an individual stylist who achieved freedom over the studio through existential choice. But the auteur was more important than the genre … the *Cahiers* group always subordinated general forms to personal visions. (Naremore 1998: 26–7)

And sure enough, two *Cahiers* critics soon made films – Jean-Luc Godard's *À bout de souffle* (1960) and François Truffaut's *Tirez sur la pianiste* (1960) – redolent of film noir but conceived as personal visions.

In 1945, American critic Lloyd Shearer described a recent 'trend in Hollywood toward the wholesale production of lusty, hard-boiled, gut-and-gore crime stories, all fashioned on a theme with a combination of plausibly motivated murder and studded with high-powered Freudian implication' (1999: 9), consisting of *Double Indemnity, Murder, My Sweet, Laura, Conflict* (1945) and the forthcoming *The Dark Corner* (1946), *The Big Sleep* (1946), *The Brasher Dubloon* (1947), *The Postman Always Rings Twice, Lady in the Lake* (1947), *The Blue Dahlia* and *Serenade* (an adaptation of Cain's 1937 novel which eventually appeared in 1956). He explains this trend in terms of a turn to realism, liberalisation at the PCA, imitations of successful films being rushed into production and their cathartic acting-out of suppressed oedipal drives. More significantly, Lloyd Shearer and, a year later, Siegfried Kracauer, identified a cycle more-or-less consonant with film noir, even if neither of them gave it that name.

The first substantial Anglophone treatment of film noir came in Charles Higham and Joel Greenberg's *Hollywood in the Forties* from 1968. Their book remains instructive, enabling the reader to see a genre being fabricated. Their chapter entitled 'Black Cinema' evokes a film noir iconography of rain-drenched nocturnal streets, trains, elevators, cocktail bars, knocked-over standard lamps, interrogation rooms, heels clicking on pavements. It attests the impact of immigrant Austro-German filmmakers, of certain cinematographers (Lee Garmes, Tony Gaudio, Lucien Ballard, Sol Polito, Ernest Haller, James Wong Howe, John F. Seitz) and composers (Franz Waxman, Max Steiner, Miklós Rózsa, Erich Korngold). (While much has been written on film noir's visual style, its musical component remains neglected; but see Porfirio 1999 and 2001.)

However, auteurism soon replaces this discussion of genre, iconography and other creative personnel. What now seems peculiar about their selection of directors – primarily Siodmak, Fritz Lang, Otto Preminger, Michael Curtiz, Billy Wilder – is the absolute pre-eminence afforded Alfred Hitchcock for *Shadow of a Doubt* (1943), *Rope* (1948) and *The Paradine Case* (1948), only the first of which might now be considered in any way central to film noir. This change of perspective can probably be explained in terms of the parallel canonisations of Hitchcock as auteur and film noir as genre. Neither now needs the kudos the other might lend, the status of each enhanced by not necessarily being connected to the other. (This, of course, produces anomalies. For example, in many respects Hitchcock's *Vertigo* is a quintessential film noir. Based on a French pulp novel, it features an unofficial investigator investigating a mysterious woman, a carefully-orchestrated murder, a voice-over and a flashback, San Francisco as a subjective maze, expressionistic flourishes and traces of gothic melodrama; and it has been profoundly influential on neo-noir, particularly the erotic thriller. However, it is typically treated as tangential to film noir, as if auteurist discourses, combined with the industrial and aesthetic choices involved in making a colour VistaVision A-picture, categorically outweigh generic affiliations.)

Higham and Greenberg's auteurism is further demonstrated when they discuss 1940s period melodramas (see Barefoot 2001): *King's Row* (1941), *The Lodger* (1944), *Gaslight* (1944), *Hangover Square* (1945), *Temptation* (1946), *Ivy* (1947) and *So Evil My Love* (1948) 'reflect the proper ambience but for the most part fail to disclose the kind of strong personal attitude which could have raised them to the level of works of art' (1970: 31). It is not insignificant that the studios, as well as 1940s and 1960s audiences, would have perceived them as 'women's pictures', or that detailed treatment is reserved for the one directed by George Cukor, who did appear in lists of possible auteurs, usually to be rejected.

Intriguingly, Higham and Greenberg deal with many film noirs in other chapters. While many films that would now be considered melodramas are treated as 'women's pictures', the 'Melodrama' chapter focuses almost exclusively on film noirs. Beginning with the claim that 'A wry detachment, an amused view of the subject ... are the qualities of the best 1940s melodramas. The films were made by hard-bitten men who knew city life inside out' (1970: 39), it examines various film noirs, including adaptations of Hammett, Chandler and Graham Greene, *Gilda* (1946), *Sorry, Wrong Number* (1948), *The Big Clock* (1948), *Caught* (1949), *The Reckless Moment* (1949), *Force of Evil* (1949) and *The Set-Up* as well as Hitchcock's *Rebecca* (1940), *Suspicion* (1941) and *Notorious*. However, Higham and Greenberg acknowledge no similarities between these films and the preceding chapter's 'black' films and women-in-peril melodramas, and they discuss other film noirs as 'problem and sociological films' and 'women's pictures'. (Higham and Greenberg's construction of 1940s Hollywood genres so as to privilege certain directors betrays the masculinist assumptions of a nascent Film Studies. Frank Krutnik (1991) offers a contrasting approach which is informative about the development of Film Studies in the intervening decades. Not only does he recognise gender problematics, but he also divides film noirs into more coherent, if overlapping and interacting, cycles of 1940s crime films with tangible connections to their production and initial distribution, exhibition and consumption.)

Raymond Durgnat's 'Paint It Black: The Family Tree of *Film Noir*' from 1970 begins by trying to elevate film noir to high art, comparable to Euripides, Goya, Dostoyevsky, Faulkner, Greek tragedy, Jacobean drama, Romanticism and, less pretentiously, to French, Italian and British cinema. He insists that film noir should be classified by 'motif and tone' (1996: 84) and is, therefore, not a genre in the way that gangster films and westerns are. While he is correct to say that not all crime films are film noirs, his suggestion that film noirs can be found in other genres is undermined by his examples, which include *King Kong* (1933) and *2001: A Space Odyssey* (1968). While few would deny the potential benefits of considering *Der Blaue Engel* (1930), *Attack* (1956) and *Sweet Smell of Success* (1957) in the light of film noir, he offers no coherent reason for claiming them for the genre; and his subsequent typology/genealogy of film noir focuses almost exclusively on crime films, effectively countering his grander claims.

Durgnat divides three hundred film noirs by cycle or motif into eleven incommensurate categories. Social criticism films examine issues like pro-hibition-era gangsters, miscarried or corrupt justice, juvenile delinquency, boxing and other rackets, and include postwar documentary-thrillers and more general indictments of American society, like *Ace in the Hole* (1951). The gangster cycles include films nostalgic for the 1930s gangster, films in which gangsters become heroes fighting Nazis or Communists, heist and caper thrillers, and films about organised crime. Other groups of films feature: criminals or innocents on the run; private eyes and adventurers; middle-class murder; portraits and doubles as symbols of paranoia and split personalities; straight and queer sexual pathologies; psychopaths; criminals holding individuals, families or other groups hostage; and Nazis or Communists portrayed as gangsters. Durgnat's final category contains guignol, horror and fantasy films about paranoia, entrapment, death, desire and alienation. For all its faults, this early charting of noir's terrain offers insights into the matrix from which current understandings of film noir grew.

Paul Schrader's 1972 'Notes on Film Noir' reiterates Durgnat's con-tention that film noir is not a genre because it 'is not defined, as are the western and gangster genres, by conventions of setting and conflict but rather by the more subtle qualities of tone and mood' (1996: 99). However, while arguing that 'Film noir is also a specific period of film history, like German Expressionism or the French New Wave' (ibid.), he describes it in terms of setting and conflict as 'Hollywood films of the 1940s and early 1950s which portrayed the world of dark, slick city streets, crime and cor-ruption' (1996: 100). His claim that 'most every dramatic Hollywood film from 1941 to 1953 contains some noir elements' (ibid.) is unsupported by anything resembling evidence, but it does return us to the dilemma of how to delimit a genre, to the question of semantic and syntactic approaches. In Schrader's words, 'How many noir elements does it take to make a film noir?' (ibid.). Side-stepping this question, he identifies wartime and postwar disillusion, a postwar interest in realism, the influence of German and East European émigré filmmakers and hard-boiled crime fiction as the four circumstances which prompted film noir production in 1940s Hollywood. He also points to some recurring stylistic techniques: lighting even daytime scenes as if it were night-time; compositional preferences for vertical and oblique to horizontal lines and within-the-frame tensions to physical action; equal lighting emphasis for both actors and set; romantic narration; complex chronologies; and 'an almost Freudian attachment to water' (1996: 104).

Schrader divides the main film noir cycle into three phases. The first (1941–46) centred on hard-boiled private-eye adaptations, featured star couples like Humphrey Bogart and Lauren Bacall, Alan Ladd and Veronica Lake, attracted studio-favoured directors like Michael Curtiz and Tay Garnett and was often studio-bound. The second (1945–49), dominated by a realist trend, featured 'less romantic leads like Richard Conte, Burt Lancaster and Charles McGraw' and favoured 'proletarian directors like [Henry] Hathaway, [Jules] Dassin and [Elia] Kazan' (1996: 106). The third (1949–53) was dominated by 'psychotic action and suicidal impulse', by actors like James Cagney, Robert Ryan and Lee Marvin and 'psychoanalyti-cally-inclined directors like [Nicholas] Ray and [Raoul] Walsh' (ibid.). While evocative, this oversimplified trajectory is potentially misleading. As Schrader's introductory paragraphs suggest, part of his interest in 'such relentlessly cynical' film noirs as *Kiss Tomorrow Goodbye* (1950) and *Kiss Me Deadly* (1955) is that they enable him to fabricate a narrative about Hollywood which allows him to dismiss *Easy Rider* (1969) and *Medium Cool* (1969) as naïve, romantic 'self-hate cinema' (1996: 99).

This is a far from full account of the first thirty years of film noir criti-cism. The massive exfoliation of writing on film noir since then makes it impossible to account for the second thirty years here. Instead, this chapter concludes with brief comments on key Anglophone books on film noir pub-lished since the 1970s.

The single most important intervention came with E. Ann Kaplan's edited collection *Women in Film Noir*, originally published in 1978. It treated film noir as being familiar enough to be analysed and criticised rather than described, and Christine Gledhill's contributions on *Klute* (1971) served notice that film noir criticism would no longer be constrained to the major cycle. The collection as a whole – an intersection of feminism, Marxism, Lacanian psychoanalysis and (post-)structuralism – was at the very centre of the theoretical developments then shaping Film Studies. The 1998 second edition added chapters on sexuality and race, but seemed belated, emphasising the extent to which the first edition was establishing, not following, trends. (Oliver and Trigo (2003) offers more detailed treatment of film noir's anxieties about race and sexuality.)

J. P. Telotte's *Voices in the Dark: The Narrative Patterns of Film Noir*, a careful examination of the specific conventions of the genre's distinctive narrative form, identifies 'four dominant narrative strategies or discursive formations' (1989: 12). First, most film noirs followed classical Hollywood third-person, 'objective' narration. Second, *Double Indemnity*'s critical success prompted over forty film noirs to utilise flashback narrative combined with voice-over. Third, film noirs used a subjective camera, sometimes in combination with a character's voice-over – *The Lady in the Lake* was shot almost exclusively in this manner. Fourth, the documentary-style of films like *Boomerang!* (1947) and *The Naked City* (1948) attempted a combination of the first two discursive formations, matching an objective camera with an authoritative voice-over that guided the viewer through the narrative.

Krutnik's *In a Lonely Street* combines several projects. It emphasises the relationships between film noir and hard-boiled fiction, establishes various American crime films cycles in the 1940s and 1950s, and draws on psychoanalytic and gender theory to consider the representation of masculinity in the 'tough' thriller cycle. Ian Cameron's *The Movie Book of Film Noir* (1992) collects important overviews and close critical readings of individual films. The essays in Joan Copjec's *Shades of Noir: A Reader* (1993) generally combine theoretical astuteness and complexity without forgetting to pay close attention to the films themselves.

Naremore's *More Than Night: Film Noir in its Contexts* historicises film noir, treating the term 'as a kind of mythology, problematising it by placing the films, the memories, and the critical literature in a series of historical frames or contexts' (1998: 2). It examines intellectual currents in postwar France which led to the fabrication of the genre; Hollywood censorship and blacklists; film noir in Asia, Latin America and Africa; and film noir's escape into other media. Paula Rabinowitz's *Black & White & Noir* (2002) inverts Naremore's project, treating film noir as a context for understanding American landscapes and history, while Edward Dimendberg's *Film Noir and the Spaces of Modernity* (2004) finds in film noirs a storehouse of memory, a record of the rapid postwar changes to America's urban landscape.

Hitherto, there is no major book-length study of neo-noir. While Foster Hirsch's *Detours and Lost Highways: A Map of Neo-Noir* (1999) is an expansive preliminary description of the films that might constitute neo-noir, Richard Martin's *Mean Streets and Raging Bulls: The Legacy of Film Noir in Contemporary American Cinema* (1997) is both a slimmer and a more substantial introduction. This relative dearth of material suggests the extent to which Film Studies is no longer so dependent on evoking genre to dignify its concerns, while the canonisation of certain director as 'auteurs' – note the allusions to Martin Scorsese, Edgar G. Ulmer and David Lynch in these two films – indicates Film Studies' problematic simultaneous address to both academic and popular constituencies.

The criticism discussed above provides numerous starting points for understanding film noir as an intersubjective discursive phenomenon, as a congellation of narratives about certain films told by different discursive agents at specific historical junctures. Between them, they produce an often-contradictory image of film noir as well as insights into the contexts in which they were produced. Having charted some elements of the genre's discursive fabrication, we will now turn to the films often considered as precursors of film noir, outlining potential sources in Weimar cinema, 1930s French cinema and American crime cinema and discussing specific film noirs in these contexts, always risking a 'backwards teleology' (Prawer 2002: 62) which distorts these earlier films through knowledge of a later genre to which they did not directly or necessarily give rise.

2   OUT OF THE PAST: THE PREHISTORY OF FILM NOIR

From any crime to its author there is a trail. It may be – as in this case – obscure; but, since matter cannot move without disturbing other matter along its path, there always is – there must be – a trail of some sort.
  – Dashiell Hammett (1985: 84)

Weimar cinema

Numerous Austro-German filmmaking personnel emigrated to America between the mid-1920s and the Second World War, many fleeing the Nazi regime (see Petrie 1985, Taylor 1983). A significant number, including John Alton, Curtis Bernhardt, Michael Curtiz, William Dieterle, Marlene Dietrich, E. A. Dupont, Karl Freund, Frederick Hollander, Harry Horner, Peter Lorre, Rudolph Maté, F. W. Murnau, Seymour Nebenzal, Max Ophüls, Otto Preminger, Miklós Rózsa, Hans J. Salter, Eugen Schüfftan, Steve Sekely, Douglas Sirk, Theodore Sparkuhl, Edgar G. Ulmer, Franz Waxman, Billy Wilder and Fred Zinnemann, worked on film noirs and noirish films. Two émigrés – Robert Siodmak and Fritz Lang – are absolutely central to the development of film noir.

After directing the noirish *Le Chemin de Rio* (1937), *Mollenard* (1938) and *Pièges* (1939) in France, Siodmak made ten film noirs in America: *Christmas Holiday* (1944), *Phantom Lady* (1944), *The Spiral Staircase* (1945), *The Strange Affair of Uncle Harry* (1945), *The Suspect* (1945), *The Killers*, *The Dark Mirror* (1946), *Cry of the City*, *Criss Cross* and *The File on Thelma*

Jordan (see Walker 1992b). Returning to Germany in 1954, he made the noirish *Nachts, wenn der Teufel kam* (1957) and, in Britain, *The Rough and the Smooth* (1959). In America, Lang directed 15 film noirs: *Fury* (1936), *You Only Live Once* (1937), *Man Hunt* (1941), *The Woman in the Window, Scarlet Street, Ministry of Fear* (1945), *Cloak and Dagger* (1946), *Secret Beyond the Door* (1948), *Clash By Night* (1952), *Rancho Notorious, The Blue Gardenia* (1953), *The Big Heat, Human Desire* (1954), *While the City Sleeps* (1956) and *Beyond a Reasonable Doubt* (1956). We will return to these two directors after outlining the significance of Weimar cinema to film noir.

The Weimar period (see Elsaesser 2000, Herf 1984, Kaes, Jay and Dimendberg 1994, Laquer 1974, Petro 1989, Sloterdjik 1988), from 1919 to 1933, is typically recalled as a time of rapid change in German culture: on the one hand, far-reaching political and social reforms (liberal democracy, suffrage, freedom of speech, improvements in housing and working conditions), a politicised avant-garde, a freewheeling and experimental nightlife; on the other, debauched and libertine decadence, crippling inflation, unemployment, anti-Bolshevism, anti-Semitism and resurgent traditional authoritarian conservatism. This dichotomy is evident in two early books about Weimar cinema: where Lotte Eisner's *The Haunted Screen: Expressionism in the German Cinema and the Influence of Max Reinhardt* (1952) found a revitalised German Romanticism, later hijacked and distorted by the Nazis, Siegfried Kracauer's *From Caligari to Hitler: A Psychological History of German Film* (1947) found such pre-fascist tendencies as the desire to be subordinated to authoritarian structures.

Germany was not the only country to produce expressionist films (see, for example, the Japanese film *Kurutta Ippeiji* from 1927), but film noir genealogies usually reduce Weimar cinema to German expressionism and German expressionism in turn to a catalogue of techniques including: 'foregrounded oblique objects, unbalanced compositions, irregular spatial arrangements, chiaroscuro lighting with a heavy play of shadows, an emphasis on oblique and vertical lines over the horizontal, and a fascination with reflection and reflective surfaces' (Telotte 1989: 17–18); 'high contrast, chiaroscuro lighting where shafts of intense light contrast starkly with deep, black shadows, and where space is fractured into an assortment of unstable lines and surfaces, often fragmented or twisted into odd angles' (Spicer 2002: 11–12); and 'displaced, decentred narratives, nested in frame tales, split or doubled stories, voice-overs and flashback narration'

(Spicer 2002: 12). Expressionism, however, was more than just a bunch of techniques.

Coined to describe an exhibition by Julien Auguste Hervé in Paris in 1901, 'Expressionism' was first used in Germany in the catalogue of a 1911 exhibition of Picasso, Braque and Dufy; by the end of the year it was also applied to Cézanne and Van Gogh, and in 1912 to several writers. Although Expressionists – including poets, dramatists, architects and filmmakers – did not form a coherent group, their work shares certain characteristics: contempt for stifling bourgeois society and industrial capitalism which subordinates everything to the demands of instrumental reason and material production; and a rejection of Impressionism's camouflaging both of its own lack of substance and of the harmful society concealed behind attractive surfaces. Regardless of medium,

> the Expressionist artist inclined to see himself as a prophetic visionary who was called to explode conventional reality, to break through the crust that had formed around men's psyches in order to give uninhibited *expression* to the energies there imprisoned. Unable to represent, describe or imitate the 'fallen' conventional world, the visionary artist of Expressionism aimed to abstract the objects of the everyday from their normal context, and recombine them into radiant beacons of a lost inner *Geist*. (Sheppard 1976: 277)

Although expressionist tendencies can be observed in earlier films, the German expressionist film (see Barlow 1982, Coates 1991) begins with *Das Kabinett des Dr. Caligari* (1919). Drawing on expressionist theatrical conventions for its performance styles, painted backdrops and irreal spaces, it led to a cycle of major productions – *Genuine* (1920), *Von morgens bis mitternachts* (1920), *Raskolnikov* (1923), *Schatten – Eine nächtliche Halluzination* (1923), *Orlacs Hände* (1924), *Das Wachsfigurenkabinett* (1924) – in which a foregrounded style distorted and transformed screen space. This overt stylisation served as a means of product-differentiation for both the domestic bourgeoisie and newly-reopened export markets. Central to the cycle were screenwriter Carl Mayer and set designers Robert Herlth, Erich Kettelhut, Kurt Richter and Hermann Warm.

The influence of expressionist theatre can also be observed in narratives about father/son relationships and the dangers of female sexuality;

about doppelgängers and perception; about types, not characters; about chaos, dementia and destruction. Although describing it as expressionist is problematic, in Lang's *Metropolis* (1926), the son, Freder (Gustav Frölich), comes into conflict with his father, Joh Fredersen (Alfred Abel), and descends into an underworld of regimented workers, where he is captivated by the saintly Maria (Brigitte Helm) while an identical, robotic false-Maria (Brigitte Helm) unleashes apocalyptic libidinal forces.

The number of genuinely expressionist films was small, but their influence on subsequent German cinema was strong and is evident in the more 'realistic' *Strassenfilm* (street film), like *Hintertreppe – Ein Film-Kammerspiel* (1921), *Die Strasse* (1923), *Die freudlose Gasse* (1923), *Dirnentragödie* (1927) and *Asphalt* (1928). *Strassenfilm* typically, and not unlike *Metropolis*, chart the paths of a male bourgeois descending into the dangers of the city at night and of a female proletarian trying to escape from her life in the underworld. A version of this twinned trajectory appears in *Der Blaue Engel* (although describing it as a *Strassenfilm* is a little unconventional). The self-important Professor Immanuel Rath (Emil Jannings) is captivated by Lola-Lola (Marlene Dietrich), a sexy, provocative singer at the Blue Angel beer hall. Dismissed from his job when this infatuation becomes public knowledge, he marries Lola-Lola and joins her cabaret troupe on the road. As his money runs out, he is reduced to selling salacious photographs of his wife to beer hall customers. The troupe's manager arranges a return to the Blue Angel, convinced that Rath, made up as a clown, will draw a crowd. Subjected to repeated humiliations for the entertainment of those who used to know him when he was a respected authority figure, he attacks Lola-Lola and flees to his old classroom where, degraded and alone, he dies. This narrative formula is not exclusive to the *Strassenfilm*. Variants of it occur in Thomas Hardy's fiction, and although buried in the queer subtext of Robert Louis Stevenson's *Strange Case of Dr Jekyll and Mr Hyde* (1886) it can usually be found – straightened – in adaptations. For example, in *Dr Jekyll and Mr Hyde* (1932), sexually-frustrated bourgeois Jekyll (Fredric March) meets working-class prostitute Ivy (Miriam Hopkins), played with tantalising pre-PCA near-nudity. Following their first encounter, Ivy's swinging gartered leg is superimposed over the departing doctor, connoting the erotic fascination that will unleash the murderous Hyde.

Ostensibly concerned with social problems arising from poverty and unemployment, the *Strassenfilm* is simultaneously fascinated with the underworld and illicit sexuality (such as Lola-Lola's fetishistic stage costume, exhibitions of sexual openness and ambiguity), frequently equating female sexuality with criminality (see Wager 1999). In this respect, it resembles the silent American gangster melodrama, which, combining a 'reforming morality' with titillation, 'saw the world from the perspective of middle-class protagonists who strayed from the virtuous path and crossed the tracks to "slum it" in the ghetto where they were burned by avaricious prostitutes, conquered by pimps, and lost their money to the gambling rackets' (Munby 1999: 24). Further parallels can be drawn between the female proletarians of the *Strassenfilm* and Hollywood 'fallen woman' films, especially the 'gold-digger' cycle, in which doubly-marginalised protagonists (proletarian and female) frequently used sex to access a doubly-excluding society's material rewards (see Jacobs 1991). In Hollywood, ongoing negotiations of the Production Code saw the ambitious, manipulative and sexually-available gold-digger reconfigured in subsequent cycles: Barbara Stanwyck's sleeping-her-way-to-the-top Lily Powers in *Baby Face* (1933) became the self-sacrificing eponymous mother trapped by social class in *Stella Dallas* (1937) who in turn became the fast-talking screwball con woman Jean Harrington in *The Lady Eve* (1941) and equally fast-talking screwball burlesque dancer Sugarpuss O'Shea in *Ball of Fire* (1941) became the femme fatale Phyllis Dietrichson in *Double Indemnity*.

Siodmak's Weimar films would generally be characterised as belonging to the *Kammerspielfilm* (chamber play film) or the *Milieutonfilm* (milieu talkie), genres of intimate realist melodrama which developed an 'aesthetic appropriate to the intimate and interior crisis features of modern urban life' (Munby 1999: 200). Key to the *Kammerspielfilm*'s 'intensely subjective' dramas was the development of the *enfesselte Kamera* (unchained camera); freed from the fixed tripod, this 'subjective camera projected the intimate psychology of individuals onto a world of external objects', prowling through a cramped, claustrophobic, enervated and dilapidated world, producing an 'uninterrupted visual flow' (Munby 1999: 201). Siodmak's interest in the 'prosaic and profane features of modern urban life' (Munby 1999: 205) and the 'vicious circles people get enmeshed in daily' (Munby 1999: 202) also saw him experiment with the documentarist *Neue Sachlichkeit* (New Objectivity), working with Seymour Nebenzal, Eugen Schüfftan, Edgar G. Ulmer, Billy Wilder and Fred Zinnemann on *Menschen am Sonntag* (1930).

In contrast, Lang's German films, indebted in part to Max Reinhardt's spectacular theatre, tended to the monumental, the epic and the apocalyptic, and attempted to capture some sense of a social totality. *Doktor Mabuse, der Spieler* (1922) connects the criminal underworld to high finance, government and the aristocracy, all of which are subject to the eponymous criminal genius's manipulations. A similar figure threatens the entire world in *Spione* (1928), while *M* (1931) explicitly parallels the criminals and the police as they separately organise to capture a serial child-killer. In *Metropolis*, Lang created a total world in two senses. First, there is no transition from the present to the future-city and we never venture outside, suggesting that it is not so much a metropolis as a metrocosm (see Bukatman 1993). Second, its brutally clear division between proletariat and bourgeoisie creates a visually-exaggerated image of capital's totalising logic. Lang's final 1930s German films, *M* and *Das Testament des Dr. Mabuse* (1933), turned inwards, relocating manipulating power within the pathological psyche rather than the machinations of a criminal mastermind.

Lang's German films depict determinist worlds which resemble both Expressionism's critique of industrial rationalisation and the image of capitalist modernity developed by the Frankfurt School. In the Frankfurt School's 'account of contemporary development in capitalist society' David Held identifies a 'constellation of elements' (1991: 210). Economics and politics increasingly integrate as business interests intervene in the running of the state for their own ends and the state intervenes in the economy to maintain conditions favourable to business. This integration leads to centralised instrumentalist bureaucracies and administration and to the suppression of local initiative. As instrumental reason dominates, social life becomes increasingly rationalised. The division of labour and mechanisation of tasks extends, focusing the individual on a tiny portion of the work process and denying him or her knowledge of the totality of what he or she is working on. This further isolates and alienates individuals, reducing the possibility of recognising shared experience, the basis of class consciousness:

> Domination becomes ever more impersonal. People become means
> to the fulfilment of purposes which appear to have an existence of
> their own. The particular pattern of social relations which condition
> these processes – the capitalist relations of production – are reified.
> As more and more areas of social life take on the characteristics

of mere commodities, reification is reinforced, and social relations become ever less comprehensible. Conflict centres increasingly on marginal issues which do not test the foundation of society. (1991: 211)

The world the Frankfurt School describes is captured in Lang's *mise-en-scène* of modernity (see Gunning 2000): there are motorbikes and motorcars; telephones, radios, miniature cameras and bugs; newspapers, international treaties and secret pacts; elaborate conspiracies and impeccably-choreographed heists and assassinations; hypnotists, megalomaniacs and madmen; dials, thermometers, gauges and countdowns; gambling, financial speculations and stock and currency manipulations; communications networks and dragnets; series (see Kaes 2001), parallels and concentric circles; locked doors, handcuffs, chains, bonds and other images of incarceration. These elements situate the subject in various networks, schemes and narrative developments – determinate forces out of his or her control. *Metropolis*'s corporate state is run by engineers and administrators under a single leader, Fredersen, whose office is at the centre of a web of information and whose role is homeostatic. This cyberneticisation is even more pronounced among the workers beneath the city. Identically-clothed diminutive figures reduced to sets of rhythmic movements, their work involves the monitoring and regulation of an abstract system. Workers on the M-Machine are mere components, human thermostats steam-scalded by this disciplinary apparatus if they fail to regulate it properly. When Freder subjects himself to the Paternoster machine, he must move the hands on this giant clock-like device so that they point at the lights around its rim as they light up in apparently random order. There is no clue to the machine's function, but its metaphorical purpose is made clear when a clock face is superimposed over it. Throughout Lang's German films clocks, watches and clock-like images (notably the children's game at the start of *M*) repeatedly signify the rationalisation of time, one of capitalist modernity's interlocking systems of subjection. (Paul Monaco offers a more specific interpretation, arguing that the clock motif in Weimar films 'represents impending danger or disaster' because of its connection with the notion of *Zeitgewinn* (winning time) underpinning Germany's military strategy: once the 1914 offensive 'fizzled, and the war became one of attrition, Germany was ... against the time factor. Her military system was not fitted for an extended war. Germany

FIGURE 1 Against the clock: *Metropolis*

had pushed for war in 1914 because it was felt that her chances of winning an inevitable war were running down with time' (1976: 30).)

Theodor Adorno and Max Horkheimer, two major Frankfurt School critics, are frequently criticised for overemphasising the integration of modern societies 'in which every element is increasingly tailored to fit into the whole, in which every aspect has its place, and in which any form of deviance or incipient criticism is either normalised or excluded' (Thompson 1990: 106). However, their work often reveals a rather more dialectical process – involving powerful systems and frequently isolated subjects, in which no victory is permanently won – which resembles a curtailed version of Antonio Gramsci's model of hegemony as negotiated-subordination (see Gramsci 1998). *Metropolis*'s conclusion offers an image of such hegemony: Maria persuades the head (Joh Fredersen) and the hands (the workers) to accept the mediation of the heart (Freder, with whom Maria has fallen in love). Although this ludicrous solution has been mocked by everyone, Lang included, it is the one for which we have generally settled: negotiation between exploiter and exploited classes (often represented as individuals rather than social classes), undertaken by proxies who ultimately function as part of the apparatus for maintaining existing economic processes. Although Lang's German and American films depict a determinist universe, he clearly perceives existence within such a universe as if not dialectical then at least agonistic, even if he prefers more metaphysical terminology:

> I think that is the main characteristic, the main theme that runs through all my pictures – this fight against destiny, against fate. I once wrote … that the fight is important – not the result of it, but the revolution itself. Sometimes, maybe, with a strong will, you can change fate, but there is no guarantee that you can. If you just sit still, however, and say, 'Well, I cannot do anything –' bang! At least, you have to fight against it. (Lang quoted in Bogdanovich 1997: 191)

Reworked in an American context, this fatalist version of determinism – central not only to Lang's and Siodmak's work but to Weimar culture more generally – continued to depict the subject as lacking agency in the face of forces beyond his or her control. Despite their differences, Siodmak and Lang contributed expressionist visions of capitalist urban modernity and 'shared in the development of a cinematic *Angstkomplex* regarding subject-power relations in modern society' (Munby 1999: 208) – which is as much Weimar's legacy for film noir as its distortions of *mise-en-scène*.

Jonathan Munby argues that because they were Americanised in the 1930s, many émigrés strongly identified with 'the ideals their adopted nation stood for during the Depression (and the war)' and thus 'were particularly disappointed by Hollywood's acquiescence to political conservatism after the war' and the 'deferment of New Deal-era promises' (1999: 212, 214). Their film noirs can, then, be regarded as palimpsests, as overwriting fatalist Weimar sociopsychology and expressionist aesthetics onto the American crime film; this can be seen in Lang's *Scarlet Street* (see Jacobowitz 1992).

Walking home from a party at which he was presented with a watch to celebrate 25 years of faithful service, cashier Christopher Cross (Edward G. Robinson) 'rescues' Kitty March (Joan Bennett) from an attacker. Infatuated, he does not correct her when she persuades herself that he is a famous and wealthy painter. Her attacker – really her boyfriend, Johnny Prince (Dan Duryea) – convinces her to lead Chris on. Unhappy at home, and repeatedly compared unfavourably by his wife to her dead first husband, Chris embezzles money so that he can set Kitty up in an expensive apartment where he can also go to paint. Johnny begins to sell Chris's paintings, signed by Kitty; when Chris finds out he insists that she continue to put her name to them. When his wife's first husband turns up alive, Chris leaves her to marry Kitty, but he finds her with Johnny. After Johnny leaves, Chris returns to her apartment and murders her. Circumstantial evidence (and a lie from Chris) condemn Johnny. He is executed, and Chris is driven mad by the thought of Kitty and Johnny united in death. He ends up, six or seven years later, a vagrant who keeps trying to confess to the police. In the final scene, he passes an art dealer where Kitty's 'self-portrait' has just been sold for $10,000. As he wanders down the street, the passers-by fade out, leaving him utterly alone, a broken man.

Munby sees in *Scarlet Street* a 'paranoid psychosexual mediation of sociohistorical change rooted in Weimar cinema' grafted onto 'less candid and more humorous pre-Code American traditions' (1999: 197). Unlike the ethnically-defined gangsters Robinson played in *Little Caesar* (1930) and *Key Largo* (1948), Chris is 'trapped in a different ghetto: the prison of bourgeois rectitude where any transgression of bourgeois morality leads one into a realm of psychotic self-punishment' (Munby 1999: 198). Likewise, Kitty transforms the gold-digging fallen woman. No serial seductress trying to climb out of tawdry circumstances, she describes her desire for Johnny – a man who beats, abuses and pimps for her – as love, and does all she can to keep his interest, such as it is. The direct social criticism found in some fallen women films is here psychologised. When Chris asks Kitty if he can paint her, she agrees, holding out her foot and nail polish. The ensuing eroticised humiliation of Chris is a role-reversed replay of her relationship with Johnny and a sadomasochistic sexual fantasy which functions as a powerful, personalised metaphor of a negotiated, and often complicit, subordination to domination. In it, one can see both Weimar sociopsychology and aesthetics and American narrative and cinematic traditions; one can see a palimpsest being written.

French cinema of the 1930s

In addition to *Le Dernier tournant* (1939), the first adaptation of Cain's *The Postman Always Rings Twice*, France also produced a number of other films that were remade in America as film noirs or noirish films – *La Chienne* (1931) as *Scarlet Street*; *Pépé le moko* (1936) as *Algiers* (1938) and *Casbah* (1948); *La Bête humaine* (1938) as *Human Desire*; *Le Jour se lève* (1939) as *The Long Night* (1947); *Pièges* as *Lured* (1947). France provided temporary sanctuary and employment for Austro-German émigrés, including Lang, Maté, Max Ophüls, Siodmak, Schüfftan, Sparkuhl, Waxman and Wilder, but as German invasion threatened, they fled to the US, along with several French filmmakers who later worked on film noirs, such as Jean Renoir, Julien Duvivier and Jacques Tourneur. However, France's main influence on film noir is typically described in terms not of personnel but of 'poetic realism'.

Coined by Jean Paulhan to describe Marcel Aymé's novel *La Rue sans nom* (1929), 'poetic realism' was later applied to its 1933 adaptation by a reviewer who described the film as 'inaugurat[ing] an entirely new genre' (Andrew 1995: 11). Overtly stylised, these stories of marginality, criminality, loyalty, betrayal and doomed romance, typically set in working-class Paris, attempt to elicit the lyrical from the quotidian. *Sous les toits de Paris* (1930), *Le Grand jeu* (1933), *La Maternelle* (1933), *L'Atalante* (1934) predate the main cycle, which ran from 1935 to 1939, and included *La Belle équipe* (1936), *Pépé le moko*, *La Bête humaine*, *Hôtel du Nord*, *Quai des brumes* and *Le Jour se lève*.

Poetic realism's roots can be traced back through contemporary crime writer Georges Simenon to nineteenth-century writers like Emile Zola, Honoré de Balzac and Eugene Sue. While some have argued that poetic realism was merely bourgeois melodrama transposed onto the proletariat, this would require it to represent the working class 'in the same patronising light' as Zola, who constantly implied 'that the working class [was] "less" than the bourgeoisie' (Hayward 1993: 148). However, as Susan Hayward argues, 'the plethora of images of male friendship, the presence of popular songs, the meticulous attention to the whole of the working-class [setting and situation] attest differently' (1993: 148). Unsurprisingly, then, poetic realism is often seen as somehow related to the rise and fall of the Popular Front, a left-wing coalition of traditionally antagonistic socialist, communist and other radical groups formed to combat the rise of fascism. Narrowly elected in 1936, they attempted to reverse

> the conservative programme of preceding years: instead of giving priority to the economic sector and attempting to balance the budget by reducing expenditure, [they] proposed a series of social

reforms involving significant public sector expenditure – the dole, public works, agricultural subsidies, and above all the reduction of the working week to forty hours – intending that these social measures should in turn trigger an economic recovery. (Crisp 1993: 4)

The Popular Front also prompted wide-ranging cultural experimentation, including films by Renoir, Duvivier and Jacques Becker (see Strebel 1980, Vincendeau and Reader 1986). The Popular Front government's pro-worker policies – introducing paid holidays and the forty-hour week, nationalising the railways, supporting unionisation – could not prevent a wave of strikes and a recession led to its collapse in October 1938. Poetic realism's fatalism has been linked to the Popular Front's *reactive* formation (in order to *oppose* fascism's growing popularity) and its inability to sustain an *active* reformist programme. Regardless of the legitimacy of such claims, two things are certain: in November 1940, poetic realist films 'were condemned and banned under legislation relating to the cleansing and regulation of the film market' (Crisp 1993: 60), and poetic realism's culminating example, *Les Enfants du paradis* (1943–45), was backward-looking, demonstrating that it belonged to an earlier conjuncture.

Colin Crisp locates poetic realism within a broader tendency between 1930 and 1950, a 'theoretically articulated and systematically implemented poeticisation which aimed not to *capture* reality but to *transpose* it' and which drew upon 'surrealist pictorial and montage techniques [and] expressionist acting, lighting and cinematography techniques' (1993: 320–1). Dudley Andrew calls poetic realism the 'mongrel whelp' of 'naturalism, impressionism and Surrealism, of those aspiring to create a refined cinema and those eager to maintain the popularity that makes cinema the art of the century' (1995: 50), and quotes Jean Mitry's description of it as an 'attenuated expressionism inserted into the norms and conditions of the immediately real where symbolism is reduced to things, to objects' (1995: 15). Unlike Hollywood's perpetual investment 'in maximum shock effects, in bursts of song, violence, eros or language', poetic realism 'diffuses such energy in a warm mist of style that mutes the sound and brightness of every effect, even as it washes over us and seeps down to the roots of feeling' (1995: 6). Although film noir replicated poetic realism's sombre nocturnal settings, glistening rain-drenched streets, swirls of fog, evocative sets and deep visual fields segmented by patterns of light and dark, it generally conveyed a different mood or tone. Poetic realism's attention to social context and the unremarkable everyday circumstances which lead to disaster tends to produce sympathy for its doomed protagonists, whereas Hollywood's emphasis on action over contemplation, exhibition over introspection, clear motivation over ambiguous, fitful promptings, tends to produce curiosity about what exactly characters will do next – a contrast best evoked by comparing *La Bête humaine* with *Double Indemnity*.

The blood of train driver Jacques Lantier (Jean Gabin) is tainted by generations of alcoholic ancestors. Prone to depression, he has fits of inchoate rage when sexually aroused, becoming a murderous automaton. After assaulting a woman he loves, he refuses her offer of marriage, believing it would end in tragedy. Deputy station-master Roubaud (Fernand Ledoux), married to the much younger Séverine (Simone Simon), discovers that Grandmorin (Berlioz), her wealthy godfather, who might actually be her father, has certainly been her lover. Roubaud forces Séverine to arrange a meeting with Grandmorin and murders him. Lantier sees Roubaud and Séverine leaving the crime scene, but her pleading eyes persuade him not to betray them. Lantier falls in love with her but, remembering his illness, agrees to be just friends. They do, however, become lovers. Séverine, bound to the increasingly-morose Roubaud by their crime, cannot leave her husband. When Lantier proves incapable of murdering Roubaud, the disappointed Séverine, convinced that Roubaud will soon kill her, breaks up with Lantier. To win her back, Lantier again sets out to kill Roubaud, but Séverine's passionate embrace triggers a fit and he stabs her to death. Next day, he hurls himself from his train and dies.

Throughout, Lantier and Séverine's actions are mitigated, at least in part, by their circumstances and lack of calculation. Séverine's involvement with Grandmorin, who has a reputation for forcing himself on women (including, possibly, her mother), is reluctant; it is implied that she married Roubaud to escape him. An unwitting and unwilling accomplice after the fact, she did not murder anyone. Despite her questionable motivation for befriending Lantier, she does fall in love with him. Likewise, Lantier is not responsible for his illness, and tries to avoid situations which might unleash the dangerous automaton he becomes during his fits.

In contrast, insurance salesman Walter Neff (Fred MacMurray) sets out cold-bloodedly to murder Dietrichson (Tom Powers) because he is physically attracted to Dietrichson's wife, Phyllis (Barbara Stanwyck); because of the insurance money; and, most importantly, because he wants to outsmart claims investigator Barton Keyes (Edward G. Robinson). Phyllis is equally calculative: she murdered Dietrichson's first wife so as to marry him, but now he is worth more to her dead. Told in flashback as Neff, bleeding to death, confesses all to Keyes' dictaphone, the film marginalises the murderers' bloodless passion in favour of a fascinated observation of their crime. As Keyes closes in, Neff realises that to get away with the original murder he must kill Phyllis. Instead, they shoot and kill each other.

La Bête humaine opens with Lantier's approach to Le Havre, parallel railtracks racing towards and beneath his train; running without deviation along a predetermined route, it metaphorises Lantier's condition and fate. After killing Séverine, he wanders off, robot-like, into the night, along a railway line. For him, there is no escape; but, significantly, that lack of escape runs in both directions – at no point in the past did he set himself on the path he must follow. In *Double Indemnity*, deterministic and machinic images and metaphors recur – from the insurance company's ranks of identical desks and Keyes' statistical tables to the railtracks where Dietrichson's body is dumped and the regular grooves of the dictaphone cylinder recording Neff's confession. Neff says the murder plan must be 'perfect ... straight down the line', and later claims that 'the machinery had started to move and nothing could stop it', that Fate had 'thrown the switch'. Keyes describes the killers as being on a 'trolley-ride together'; unable to 'get off at different stops', they are 'stuck with each other and they've got to ride all the way to the end of the line, and it's a one-way trip and the last stop is the cemetery'. Thanks to the ingenious casting of MacMurray, one might feel some sympathy for Neff. From his first encounter with Phyllis he is out of his depth while imagining he is in control – in the novel, he says 'I loved her like a rabbit loves a rattlesnake' (Cain 2002: 84), but in the film he lacks this self-knowledge. However, the flashback structure counters any sympathy developing, generating not a sense of foreboding but the certainty of Neff's failure. If *La Bête humaine*'s unfolding plot makes one wonder 'what will happen to these poor people next?', *Double Indemnity*'s retrospective structure prompts the sharper query, 'how exactly did he bring this upon himself?'

This different tone is not an inevitable by-product of the flashback structure. *Le Jour se lève* opens with François (Jean Gabin) killing Valentin (Jules Berry), and his apartment being surrounded by armed police. In the first of three flashbacks, François meets Françoise (Jacqueline Laurent). Born on

FIGURE 2 Out of his depth: *Double Indemnity*

the same day, named after the same saint and raised in orphanages, they are both depicted as childlike – François drinks milk, Françoise has a teddy bear called Bolop. They soon fall in love, but from the outset one knows their love is doomed: when Françoise first enters François' factory, fumes kill her flowers; and in the opening sequence Bolop is hit by police gunfire. Françoise is involved with an older man, Valentin, who has a performing-dogs act. François is picked up by Valentin's assistant Clara (Arletty), who has just quit the act. In the second flashback, set two months later, François and Clara are lovers and Françoise and Valentin seem to be. Pretending that he is Françoise's father, Valentin tries to stop François from seeing her. Françoise assures François that Valentin was lying, and they both promise to stop seeing the others. François, however, becomes convinced that, despite her denials, Françoise has been Valentin's lover. In the third flash-back, Valentin visits François, intending to kill him. Valentin goads François by implying a sexual relationship with Françoise. François takes Valentin's gun and shoots him. Back in the present, François kills himself. Despite sharing a flashback structure similar to *Double Indemnity*'s, the tone of the film is closer to that of *La Bête humaine* because François' memories reveal emotion, passion, misinterpretation and events beyond control rather than a process of calculation.

Although told without flashbacks or poetic realism's expressionist techniques, *Pépé le moko* shares something of this tone by making the protagonists victims of calculation. It opens in Algiers two years after the heist which forced Pépé (Jean Gabin) to flee France (on *Pépé le moko* as a colonialist fantasy, see Morgan 1997, O'Shaughnessy 1996; on film noir's use of exotic locales, see Naremore 1998). His Casbah hideout has become like a prison to him. Watching ships sail from the harbour, he yearns for Paris. His appearance and behaviour capture his awkward, interstitial position. Eschewing Parisian working-class costume, Pépé combines a proletarian physique and physiognomy with a natty dress-sense, evoking the 1930s Hollywood consumer-gangster but without the mobster's brashness (see Vincendeau 1998: 41–9). As dapper as a gentleman-thief, his class origin denies him the panache of Raffles or Arsène Lupin.

Pépé falls in love with Gaby (Mireille Balin), the mistress of champagne magnate Kleep (Charles Granval). She is made-up, costumed and lit so as to emphasise the contrast between her European whiteness and the dark, uncertain ethnicity of Pépé's gypsy lover, Inès (Line Noro). Raised in the same neighbourhood as Pépé, Gaby misses Paris too. She leaves Kleep for Pépé, but Inspector Slimane (Lucas Gridoux) tells her that Pépé has been killed. Kleep, intent on leaving Algiers, takes her back. Pépé is distraught when Gaby misses their rendezvous. Slimane almost tricks him into going to Gaby's hotel, where it will be easy to arrest him. Pépé learns of Gaby's imminent departure. Shots of Pépé running through the Casbah set are replaced by shots of him running in front of back-projected streets. Behind him, one shot dissolves into another, the last one not of buildings but of surging, crashing waves – a brief eruption of expressionist artifice as his passion overcomes any trace of calculation. Tipped off by Inès, Slimane arrests Pépé as he is about to join Gaby aboard ship. Handcuffed behind the prison-like bars of the harbour gates, Pépé calls out to Gaby as she appears on deck, but the ship's klaxon drowns out his voice. He kills himself.

Pépé and Gaby are calculative in their relationships with others, but in their romance emotion and compassion overwhelm instrumentalism. Pépé invests Gaby with all his longings – just as he does with Paris, the sea and the ships that sail upon it – and Gaby sees in him an alternative to her life of, effectively, prostitution. This is tempered by their recognition of each other's entrapment and the identification, manifested as passion-ate romantic love, it prompts. Reworking *Strassenfilm* and Hollywood gold-digger-film logic, a proletarian couple, having found differently-gendered routes (crime and sex) to material well-being, are denied a redemptive return to their proletarian origins.

The difference in tone between French poetic realism and American film noir largely derives from differing conceptions of agency. *Double Indemnity* opens with Neff racing to his office where he will record his confession. In long shot, his car races towards us, following the dead-straight parallel lines of streetcar tracks. In the foreground, a maintenance crew is working on the lines. The car swerves around them and rushes on, jumping a stop-sign. This sequence seems like a direct riposte to the opening of *La Bête humaine*, described above, in which Lantier cannot deviate from the rail-tracks laid down before him. Each of the poetic realist films here described, regardless of whether or not they have a flashback structure, both depict and tell a fatalistic world, but *Double Indemnity* opens up a gap between determinism and fatalism, depiction and telling. It depicts a determinist world, but Neff's telling of it is not fatalist. His flashback narration prevents a poetic realist conflation of determinism and fatalism. Just as he veers off the streetcar tracks and onto a fresh path, so he believes that he can escape the consequences of his actions (or, more accurately, act in such a way that certain of his actions do not have certain consequences); if only he can kill Phyllis, if only he can get to Mexico...

All of these films are fantasies about the possibility of agency. The poetic realist films regard agency as either illusory or irrelevant: regardless of what you do while you are on the train, it is still going to pull into the same station. In *Double Indemnity* and other film noirs, the protagonists lay the tracks themselves.

1930s Hollywood crime films

At night, in long shot, a car pulls up at a rural gas station, a circle of light in a black frame. Figures leap out and rush into the building. The light goes out. Gunshots, muzzle-flashes. The sound of a cash-register. This minimalist exercise in light and sound opens *Little Caesar*, the first major entry in Hollywood's 1930s gangster cycle. In the following scene, Caesar Enrico Bandello (Edward G. Robinson), bemoaning the lack of opportunity for criminal advancement in the sticks, resolves to head for the big city; his partner, Joe (Douglas Fairbanks, Jr), who wants to resume his dancing career, imagines the new clothes he will buy. These two scenes establish the cycle's central characteristics. Rejecting rural associations with the past and the models of criminality offered by westerns and dust-bowl outlaws like Dillinger and Bonnie and Clyde, it embraces capitalist modernity as figured by the city. Productive labour is dismissed in favour of leisure and consumption. This idea of consumption-as-utopian-goal (see Moylan 1986) is reiterated visually when a mobster's jewellery is subjected to Caesar's gaze in the kind of shot usually reserved for eroticising the female body. Caesar's frequent costume changes and his belief that a painting cost $15,000 because of its 'gold frame' further develops the idea of consumption-as-spectacle. Finally, we are introduced to troubled masculinities: Caesar is uninterested in women, while Joe is 'feminised' as a dancer – later, a jealous Caesar threatens to kill Joe's girlfriend as they compete for Joe's attention.

The Public Enemy (1931) replicates Little Caesar's rise-and-fall narrative. It begins with aerial shots of the city, the stockyards and streets, cruising an intersection before settling on two boys, Tommy Powers (James Cagney) and a friend, the camera analogous to the Strassenfilm's bourgeois descending into the underworld. Tommy's law-abiding brother works in low-paid jobs, studies at night, marries his childhood sweetheart, enlists in the army, slowly recovers from shell-shock, returns to low-paid work; Tommy turns to crime instead. He, too, undergoes sartorial transformations, but while Caesar is merely uninterested in women, Tommy is impotent.

If not expressionist, both films deploy expressive mise-en-scène. In Little Caesar, long shots of rooms often feature emphatic diagonal lines, some explicitly moderne. The Public Enemy frequently situates Tommy among strong vertical lines, associated with his rise, but when he is shot, he falls in a rain-filled gutter, is prostrated in a hospital bed; when kidnappers return him, he is bound and trussed, upright in the doorway – and then he falls flat on his face, dead.

Scarface (1932), based on Armitage Trail's 1930 novel (itself a catalogue of gangster fiction tropes), also follows a mobster's rise and fall. Tony Camonte's (Paul Muni) ascent is marked by the accumulation and display of commodities; his demise stems from an incestuous desire for his sister. The artifice of Scarface's opening low-angle shot presages a thoroughly noirish visual style. Notable by its absence from the brightly-lit inserted sequence, shot by someone else, in which civic spokespeople deplore the gangster phenomenon, it is particularly conspicuous in the repetition of X-shapes when characters are killed. Only occasionally diegetically-motivated, the repetition of X-shapes creates a consistently fatalist world – whenever an X appears, someone dies – which counterpoints the commodity's false utopianism. Camonte's death belies the Cooks Tours' neon billboard, which promises 'The World is Yours'. He has been, at best, a tourist amid wealth and power. He is gunned down by the socially-sanctioned agents of determinate class and ethnic structures.

As Munby argues, part of these films' significance is that in them the gangsters *talked* and did so with voices of distinct ethnic and class origins. Jewish-American and Irish-American actors playing powerful, charismatic Italian-American and Irish-American characters celebrated non-WASP identities while drawing attention to class- and ethnicity-based social exclusions. Despite their reactionary ghettoisation of crime, they gave voices to excluded Americans: 'A space of cultural containment and ideological legitimation was turned into something more rebellious' (1999: 5), simultaneously recapitulating, through costume and decor, images of capitalist excess while dramatising the exclusionary practices and processes faced by ethnicised and other workers. (Similar processes can be observed in Blaxploitation and New Jack Cinema.)

For C. L. R. James, gangster films exemplified the increasingly apparent fissure between capitalist modernity and an outmoded national self-image:

> The gangster did not fall from the sky ... He is the persistent symbol of the national past which now has no meaning – the past in which energy, determination, bravery were certain to get a man somewhere in the line of opportunity. Now the man on the assembly line, the farmer, know that they are there for life; and the gangster who displays all the old heroic qualities in the only way he can display them, is the derisive symbol of the contrast between ideals and reality. (1993: 127)

This fissure is more pronounced in *High Sierra* and *White Heat*, film noirs which cast actors with urban associations from 1930s crime cinema as gangsters-out-of-time in stories which recall rural outlaws. (The gangster-out-of-time also appears in *Key Largo* and *His Kind of Woman* (1951) as an irrational force returning and disturbing an orderly America.)

After eight years in prison, *High Sierra*'s Roy Earle (Humphrey Bogart) makes straight for a park, to make sure 'grass is still green and trees are still growing', rather than the city. Explicitly compared to Dillinger, he is anachronistic: his old boss is dying and younger hoods regard him as legendary. The owners of his family's old farm are worried he is from the bank, and, in an even more obvious allusion to the Depression-era outlaw, he befriends a California-bound family of bankrupt farmers. Moreover, Earle's dark suit seems out of place in the west coast's bright sunshine and more horizontal than vertical cities. Eventually cornered by police surveillance and communications technologies, Earle makes his last stand on Mount Witney – it is broadcast by radio to the nation – and is shot by a character in western costume.

White Heat opens with a steam train hold-up and ends with a shoot-out in an ultra-modern chemical plant. In between, Cody Jarrett (James Cagney), often costumed as a more rural than urban figure, is rarely seen in a fully urban setting. Like Earle, Cody is ill-suited to the city, his past-ness emphasised by his 'fierce psychopathic devotion' to his mother (the headaches and fits which, in childhood, he faked to get her attention, have now become real). He challenges the tendency to see the rational modern world as rigidly determinist. This rationality is evoked by images of order – for example, the co-ordination of various agencies' resources to triangulate the radio signal which will give away Cody's position, a process initially demonstrated diagramatically and then presented in a procedural montage sequence – and is challenged by contingency and disorder. Treasury agents follow a grid-like city map as they tail Ma Jarrett (Margaret Wycherly), losing her then relocating her by chance; the ordered ranks of the prison dining hall are thrown into temporary disarray by Cody's violent fit; the elaborate scheme to allow Cody's escape is abandoned because of this fit, only for him to escape anyway. Cody completes his transition from idealised western past to rational modern world, going beyond the city to a location which seems futuristic, and there, deranged, unleashes an irrational, apocalyptic explosion. (See Corber 1997 on film noir's nostalgia for pre-Fordist capitalism.)

Such films expunge the ethnic and working-class identities and contexts of the 1930s gangster cycle, focusing instead on crime as an endemic national condition (both hint at vast unseen criminal organisations) and on individualised psychology (Earle's embodiment of *thanatos*, Cody's mother fixation). As exemplified by *White Heat*, film noir's recurrent conflict between the rational and the irrational sees the apparently determinist world disrupted, only for these disruptions to be revealed as arising from other determinants which were not taken into account: plans go awry, murder plots and minutely-planned heists go wrong, individuals refuse subordination to the gangster-corporation, coincidences and contingencies betray, but a new (narrative) order emerges. Embedded in many film noirs is a clear sense of the inadequacy of models of linear determinism. Narratives arise from the collision of different presumed linearities, hinting at the nonlinear determinism of emergent complex systems.

Genealogical overviews of film noir typically reduce 1930s Hollywood crime films to the gangster cycle initiated by *The Doorway to Hell* (1930) and ended by the 1935 Hays Office moratorium on gangster films. Yet as early as 1930, Harry Potamkin identified another cycle of crime films, including *Underworld* (1927), *Street of Chance* (1930), *Roadhouse Nights* (1930) and *Ladies Love Brutes* (1930), which by various means, such as 'reducing the themes of gang strife to a love triangle', shift and dissipate the 'burden of social guilt' (1977: 477). He considered this cycle 'part of America's celebration of her corruption' (1977: 478).

The early sound period also saw hard-boiled fiction influence crime film. Burnett, author of *Little Caesar*, co-scripted *The Finger Points* (1931) and provided the story for *Beast of the City* (1932). James M. Cain became a Paramount scriptwriter in 1931, before moving to Columbia; MGM bought the rights to *The Postman Always Rings Twice* in 1934 and Paramount the rights to *Double Indemnity* in 1936. Dashiell Hammett wrote the screen story for *City Streets* (1931). His 1931 *The Glass Key* and his 1934 *The Thin Man* were adapted under the same titles in 1935 and 1934, respectively, and *The Maltese Falcon* was adapted twice in the 1930s, as *The Maltese Falcon* (1931) and *Satan Met A Lady* (1936).

The success of the screwball murder-mystery *The Thin Man* led to five film sequels by 1947 and inspired a cycle of detective-couple and other comedy-mystery films, including *Remember Last Night?* (1935), *The Mad Miss Manton* (1936), *The Ex-Mrs Bradford* (1936) and *A Night to Remember* (1943). The 1930s and 1940s also produced many B-film series about detectives and crime-fighters, like Boston Blackie, Charlie Chan, Nancy Drew, Bulldog Drummond, the Falcon, the Lone Wolf, Michael Shayne, Mr Moto,

Ellery Queen, the Saint, Sherlock Holmes and Philo Vance. Several drew on hard-boiled sources: *The Falcon Takes Over* (1942) was adapted from Raymond Chandler's 1940 *Farewell, My Lovely*; Michael Shayne was taken from Brett Halliday's novels and some of his adventures were based on other hard-boiled fiction, including *Time to Kill* (1942) adapted from Chandler's 1942 *The High Window*. These series also often contained noirish elements. For example, both *The Spider Woman* (1944) and *The Woman in Green* (1945) pit Sherlock Holmes against cerebral femme fatales, and Elwood Bredell's cinematography for *Sherlock Homes and the Voice of Terror* (1942) anticipates his work on film noirs like *Phantom Lady* and *The Killers*.

A cycle centred on institutional crimefighters emerged in the mid-1930s, including *G-Men* (1935), *Bullets or Ballots* (1936), *I Am the Law* (1938) and *Racket Busters* (1938). As *G-Men* and *Bullets or Ballots* – starring, respectively, James Cagney turning against his underworld upbringing to join the FBI and Edward G. Robinson faking dismissal from the police so he can infiltrate the mob – suggest, Hollywood reworked the gangster film so that their charismatic stars and violent action were framed within the appearance of respectability; and with films like *Hard To Handle* (1933) and *Footlight Parade* (1933), Cagney's manic embodiment of capitalist urban modernity was transformed into more-or-less legal entrepreneurialism.

The Mayor of Hell (1933), *Dead End* (1937) and *Angels with Dirty Faces* (1938) ostensibly argue that crime has social causes rooted in poverty and exacerbated by institutions like reform schools. These social consciousness and sociological gestures were, of course, simultaneously undermined. *Angels with Dirty Faces* paired energetic tough-guy Rocky Sullivan (James Cagney) with saintly but dull Jerry Connolly (Pat O'Brien), childhood friends who grew up in the same environment but followed divergent paths, one turning to crime, the other to the cloth. *The Mayor of Hell*, in which Richard 'Patsy' Gargan (James Cagney) tackles the vile reform school head Mr Thompson (Dudley Digges), suggests that it is not so much institutions that are at fault as the corrupt people running them. In fact, one has to turn to *I Am a Fugitive from a Chain Gang* (1932), a pre-PCA film, to find a fairly unequivocal critique of the penal system (although this, too, contains a memorably awkward moment in which the brutal image of the chain gang presented in the rest of the film is denied, presumably in an attempt to avoid censorship in states which still used chain gangs). Ironically sharing a similar rise-and-fall narrative with early 1930s gangster film, it inverts their tacked-on crime-doesn't-pay morality to suggest that the fault lies with the systems which criminalise individuals. War veteran James Allen (Paul Muni) quits his unfulfilling factory job, becoming an itinerant labourer and then a hobo. Wrongly sentenced to hard labour for a crime he did not commit, he escapes from the chain gang. In Chicago, where he has found success working in construction, his past catches up with him. Marie (Glenda Farell) blackmails him into a loveless marriage. When he falls in love with Helen (Helen Vinson), Marie exposes him. He fights extradition, but eventually agrees to return and serve out a nominal sentence in a clerical position. The state, however, reneges upon the deal, putting him on a chain gang and indefinitely suspending his pardon. Allen escapes again and one night, a year later, he finds Helen. He emerges from the darkness to bid her a final farewell. A sound disturbs them. Edging back into the darkness, he refuses Helen's offer of money. 'How do you live?', she asks, and from a pitch black screen come the words, 'I steal', and the sound of his fleeing footsteps.

While *I Am a Fugitive from a Chain Gang* recognises the indifference and brutality of individuals within the judicial and penal systems, it does not attempt to disavow systemic indifference and brutality. Allen's initial descent into vagrancy is situated in a broader social context – he is unable to pawn his medal because the pawnbroker already has a tray full of medals pawned by other veterans. A series of visual and aural echoes highlights the carceral aspects of American society, particularly those concerning labour: Allen looking out of his office window, convicts looking through the bunkhouse window, and Allen looking through a double set of bars and mesh to talk to his brother; factory sirens and prison sirens; chains fed through convicts' shackles and the chains fed through workhorses' bridles; Allen swinging a sledgehammer on the chain gang and a pickaxe on a construction gang; a shoe factory and a labour camp. This sense of social incarceration, of inescapable determinate structures of domination, is heightened by the title's tense: *I Am*, not *I Was*.

Two of Lang's early American films, each with a noirish visual style and a sense of inescapable fate, offer variants on this theme while moving away from the social into the psychological and metaphysical. In *Fury*, Joe Wilson (Spencer Tracy), *en route* to a reunion with fiancée Katharine Grant (Sylvia Sidney), is arrested on suspicion of kidnap. Whipped into a frenzy, the townsfolk storm the gaol where he is held and burn it down. Joe escapes, but pretends to be dead so that his brothers can see his 'murderers' – whose not-

FIGURE 3 Behind bars: *Pépé le moko*

guilty pleas are undone by newsreel footage of the riot – brought to justice. Eventually, conquering his own fury, he prevents the conviction of the towns-folk for a murder they did not commit. *Fury* was inspired by the 1933 lynching in San José of two suspects in a kidnap case; California's governor endorsed the lynching and only one of the hundreds-strong lynch mob was indicted (the charges were later dismissed). Presumably because of MGM's conserva-tism, the PCA and the important markets provided by Southern states, there was never any possibility of *Fury* directly criticising the complicity of the judi-cial system in this particular crime and numerous other racially-motivated lynchings. Potential criticism of the media is also undone by the dénoue-ment: early on, newsreel cameramen keenly anticipate filming the mob in action, but in the courtroom the footage is taken as an objective record. Instead, *Fury* becomes an attack on mob psychology and revenge, both of which are depicted, as in *Metropolis* and *M*, as derangements.

In *You Only Live Once*, three-time loser Eddie Taylor (Henry Fonda) – with the aid of fiancée Joan Graham (Sylvia Sidney), her public prosecutor boss, Stephen Whitney (Barton McLane), and prison chaplain Father Dolan

(William Gargan) – is determined to go straight, but soon after he and Joan are married, he loses his job. His old gang pull off a bank robbery, killing six people and framing Eddie. Sentenced to death on circumstantial evidence, he escapes from prison, killing Dolan, who has brought news of the discovery of the real robber. On the run with the pregnant Joan, Eddie complains, like *I Am a Fugitive from a Chain Gang*'s James Allen and *Das Testament des Dr. Mabuse*'s Tom Kent (Gustav Diessl), that 'they made me a criminal'. They are shot at a police roadblock. As Eddie, carrying the dead Joan, stumbles to his death, he hears Dolan's voice, repeating the words with which he had emerged, Christ-like, from the fog in the prison yard: 'Eddie. Eddie. You're free, Eddie, the gates are open.' These final words are accompanied by an angelic chorus whose origin, diegetic or extra-diegetic, is unclear. By loading its conclusion with religious imagery – Eddie and Joan's flight with their baby alludes to the flight to Egypt – the film subordinates social criticism to a melancholy metaphysics, reinforcing the sense derived from the deliberate and ironic implausibility of the coincidences which trap Eddie and Joan that it is the universe itself, rather than particular social circumstances, that determines their fate.

With its fatalist aura, *You Only Live Once* comes closer to poetic realism than any other Hollywood film, while providing an important prototype for such couple-on-the-run film noirs as *They Live by Night* and *Gun Crazy*. It is also significant in terms of its remarkable images of entrapment – the bars that separate Eddie and Joan at their first reunion; the metal and glass which separates them in prison; the rifle-sight which frames the dying Eddie – and its noirish use of light and shadow, most notably the spider's web of shadows cast by Eddie's death-row cage. Such chiaroscuro visuals would, retrospectively, become one of the defining characteristics of film noir; and, as Marc Vernet (1993) suggests, this element of noir's visual style can be traced back not just through 1930s American crime films but also through the earlier careers, beginning in the 1910s and 1920s, of noir cinematographers like Alton, Gaudio, Seitz, Polito, Nicolas Musuraca and Joseph LaShelle, and through Hollywood gothic and horror films of the 1920s and 1930s.

David J. Skal (1993) argues that many of the horror films of the late-silent and early-sound period, especially Tod Browning's non-supernatural gothics starring Lon Chaney, are displaced articulations of the physical trauma of the First World War, particularly of the shattered, maimed and disfigured bodies of European veterans. As Hollywood horror became increasingly fantasy-based with the 1930s Universal cycle, starting with *Dracula* (1931) and *Frankenstein* (1931), and increasingly expressionist in its design and cinematography, with *The Black Cat* (1934) and *Bride of Frankenstein* (1935), so the capacity of the *mise-en-scène* to register the characters' subjective turmoil, torment and disorientation became apparent, culminating in *Cat People* (1942), in which the psychosexual anxieties of Irena (Simone Simon) seem to take on physical form. Similarly, film noir might be seen as displacing the psychological traumas of the Second World War and the dawning atomic age, with 1950s science fiction sharing horror's ability to manifest anxieties as active and monstrous elements of the *mise-en-scène*. (It is tempting then to suggest that the coincidence of the American invasion and occupation of Vietnam – and the collapse of the Cold War consensus it betokened – with the first stirrings of neo-noir and such non-supernatural horror films as *I Drink Your Blood* (1971), *The Last House on the Left* (1972), *The Crazies* (1973) and *The Texas Chain Saw Massacre* (1974) is more than a coincidence (see Bould 2003).)

We will now turn to film noir's main cycle, briefly returning to the problem of definition before examining two groups of films which will enable further discussion of determinism.

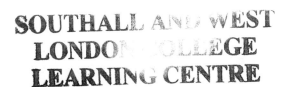

3   DARK PASSAGE: THE MAIN CYCLE OF FILM NOIR

Their characters lived in a world gone wrong, a world in which ...
civilisation had created the machinery for its own destruction and
was learning to use it with all the moronic delight of a gangster
trying out his first machine-gun.
　　　　　　　　　　　　　　　　　　– Raymond Chandler (1980: 9)

If one accepts that film noir, like any other genre, is in an ongoing process
of ultimately irresolvable discursive formation, then any generalisation
one makes about it will founder not only on multiple exceptions but also
on other versions of the genre formulated by other discursive agents. This
process of definition is one of refinement in a particular sense: it does not
refine the definition of film noir to a single formulation upon which all will
agree; rather, it promotes refinements of detail, argument and formulation
while simultaneously exfoliating them, creating further contradictions with
which to drive the process. A great many individual films and alternative
descriptions of similar and overlapping phenomena have been caught up
in the wake of this dynamic process, and so rather than attempting to make
any generalisable claims about film noir, this chapter will discuss a number
of films generally considered film noirs, grouped together as films about
entrapment and films about investigation. These are, of course, incommensurate and frequently overlapping categories. They are constructed so as to
enable an examination of the genre's recurring, but not necessarily defining, concern with determinism – a concern manifested in a more specific
critique of the determinate structures of postwar America as it entered a
late-capitalist stage.

On one level, of course, narratives about individual agency inevitably prompt questions of determinism – social, psychological, linguistic, ideological and, above all, narrative – and autonomy; and it would, therefore, be easy to subsume all film noirs to a definition focused on determinism and, from there, on subject-power relationships under capitalism. Even as this possibility points to the neglected relationship between film noir and the 1950s family melodramas of, for example, Vincente Minnelli, Nicholas Ray and Douglas Sirk, the ease of pursuing such a project indicates quite how ill-advised it would be. Such totalising braggadocio would iron out the differences and contradictions in and between films and genres. Therefore, this chapter attempts to discuss something of film noir's range and variety in relation to a particular theoretical concern without reducing them to epiphenomena of that concern.

Trapped

Images and narratives of entrapment, already evident in 1930s American cinema, become increasingly common in film noirs. Innocent men are framed, imprisoned for crimes they did not commit or caught up unwittingly in conspiracies and plots in *Stranger on the Third Floor*, *I Wake Up Screaming* (1942), *The Fallen Sparrow* (1943), *Phantom Lady*, *Crack-Up* (1946), *Dark Corner*, *Dark Passage*, *Desperate* (1947), *Out of the Past*, *The Web* (1947), *The Big Clock*, *Raw Deal* (1948), *Convicted* (1950), *Side Street* (1950), *Where the Sidewalk Ends* (1950), *His Kind of Woman*, *I Confess* (1953), *Nightfall* (1957) and *The Wrong Man* (1957). In *The Lost Weekend*, Don Birnam (Ray Milland) is trapped by alcoholism, but even more so by his failure as a writer, while in *Nightmare Alley* (1947), the descent of Stanton Carlisle (Tyrone Power) into alcoholism and carnival-freakery is variously attributed to God, the Tarot and the hubris of trying to escape poverty. This sense of entrapment becomes particularly paranoid and nightmarish in adaptations of Cornell Woolrich's fiction (see Reid and Walker 1993).

Female identity, and masculine fantasies thereof, were at the centre of a film noir cycle about wives who find themselves isolated, in danger or victims of husbands' plots. In *Suspicion* (1941) and *Beyond the Forest* (1949) the danger is imagined, but in *Experiment Perilous* (1944), *Gaslight*, *My Name is Julia Ross* (1945), *Gilda*, *Notorious*, *Undercurrent* (1946), *The Two Mrs. Carrolls* (1947), *Secret Beyond the Door*, *Sleep, My Love* (1948), *Sorry,*

Wrong Number, *Caught*, *Cause for Alarm* (1951) and *Sudden Fear* (1952) the threat is real. Women are trapped and imperilled by criminals, psychotic killers or unscrupulous men in *Hangover Square*, *The Spiral Staircase*, *The Reckless Moment*, *Beware, My Lovely* (1952) and *The Blue Gardenia*. Some of these films have period settings and most, having been perceived as 'women's pictures', have often been excluded from the film noir canon, just as discussions of melodrama have often excluded film noirs – impoverishing our understanding of both genres.

Taking a moment from *Metropolis* as its starting point, this section will consider the implications of the opening sequences of three film noirs whose subsequent combination of flashback/voice-over narrative strongly evokes a linguistic determinism (for critical treatments of linguistic determinism, see McNally 1995 and 2001, Collins 2000). It will then discuss another five film noirs which produce images and tales of entrapment and elaborate upon this sense of a foreclosed world.

Throughout *Metropolis*, Lang's camera is generally static. One of the less spectacular exceptions to this opens up the complexity of determinism once one takes into account feedback and the impossibility of closing a system to external influences. Following the explosion of the M-machine, Freder goes to Joh's office, the nerve-centre of the city. Side-by-side, father and son walk down the length of the office, facing a camera which tracks backward away from them as they move toward it. The camera starts to track back just before they begin to walk and stops just after they do; it restarts tracking back just before they start walking again, and this time stops just before they do. The interrelation of character movement and camera movement, although apparently straightforward, is actually complex: does the camera start moving before the characters and stop before they do because it is anticipating their movements, or do the characters start and stop moving in response to the camera? And when the camera stops moving after the characters, have they anticipated its movement or has it failed to anticipate theirs? In short, is character movement subject to camera movement, or vice versa? That the camera does not always anticipate the characters' movements, and that the characters on one occasion pre-empt the camera coming to a halt, is indicative of a complex determinism; the state of this system from moment-to-moment cannot be reduced to cause-and-effect. This sequence from *Metropolis* should be considered alongside the title sequences of *Detour* (1945), *Sunset Blvd.* (1950) and *D.O.A.* (1950), three film noirs made for three different studios – the 'big five' major Paramount, the 'little three' major United Artists and the 'poverty row' minor PRC (Producers Releasing Corporation) – which range from a prestigious A-picture to a low-budget B-movie shot in six days.

Sunset Blvd. opens with a shot of a sidewalk: the camera tilts down to reveal the street name on the kerb and then tracks away and into the road, always pointed downward, excluding everything else from the frame as the credits roll. At last, as director Billy Wilder's name appears, the camera tilts up to look straight back down the road as police motorcycles and cars, their sirens wailing, appear over a crest. The camera pans through 180° to follow them as they race past. As this minute-and-a-half-long shot comes to an end, Joe Gillis's (William Holden) voice-over begins, offering to tell us 'the facts, the whole truth' about how he came to be floating face-down, dead, in the swimming pool behind a former film star's mansion. He selects 'the day when it all started' about six months earlier. A failing screenwriter, he was 'grinding out original stories, two a week' that he could not sell – 'Maybe they weren't original enough, maybe they were too original'. Fleeing repo men, he turns into the driveway of silent-era star Norma Desmond (Gloria Swanson). A peculiar relationship develops, and when Joe eventually tries to leave her, she shoots him.

D.O.A., inspired by Siodmak's *Der Man, der Seinen Morder Sucht* (1931), opens with a shot that tilts down from an imposing office building at night, reaching street level as Frank Bigelow (Edmond O'Brien) enters the left of the frame and hurries across the road to the building. Dissolve to a tracking shot, the camera following Bigelow down a lengthy corridor into the Police Department. He reaches a juncture, where a cop points him down the left-hand corridor, and as he and the camera turn down it, the shot dissolves to another lengthy corridor, which Bigelow follows until he reaches a door marked Homicide Division. These two shots of Bigelow walking purposefully down two corridors whose symmetry is emphasised by his position in the middle of both the corridors and the frame, directly below the line of the ceiling lights, last for one-and-a-half minutes. Throughout, the camera maintains the same distance from his back. Bigelow has come to report his own murder, and he tells, in flashback, of being poisoned with a 'luminous toxin' which is slowly but surely killing him. When he completes the story of his investigation into the murky reasons for his assassination, he dies.

FIGURE 4   Already dead: *Sunset Blvd.*

Detour opens with an eighty-second shot of a road, filmed from the rear of a car as it drives through the desert. Unlike *Sunset Blvd.* and *D.O.A.*, this opening shot is not incorporated into the narrative. The story, remembered in flashback, follows Al Roberts (Tom Neal) as he hitchhikes from New York to Hollywood to join his girlfriend, Sue (Claudia Drake). He is picked up by Charles Haskell, Jr (Edmund MacDonald), who dies under circumstances which Al thinks will look like murder. He adopts Haskell's identity to get away, but makes the mistake of picking up Vera (Ann Savage), who had previously been given a lift by Haskell. She blackmails Al into helping her get money, plotting first to sell Haskell's car and then to collect his inheritance. When Al finally stands up to her, he accidentally kills her. He wanders off, caught in an impossible situation: if he claims to be Al, he will look guilty of Haskell's murder; if he claims to be Haskell, he will look guilty of Vera's murder; and if he tells the truth, no-one is likely to believe him. The film ends as Al is picked up by the police.

Each of these title sequences encapsulates the fatalist sensibility with which the protagonists tell the determinist world their respective films depict. *Sunset Blvd.* posits a parallel between Joe and the camera: both happen to turn into that particular road and are then swept up in a narrative. Joe regards it as mere chance that intervened six months earlier, but his retrospective narration suggests an inevitable trajectory from the driveway to the swimming pool. The contradiction in this logic stems from the narrative imposition of a finite boundary on causation. Just as Wilder's decision to start his film with that kerbstone was, ultimately, arbitrary, so is Joe's selection of that particular moment. This is not to say that these are capricious choices. They are arbitrary in that they depend upon the exercise of discretion to select a wellspring-moment; and they are arbitrary in that they become, in retrospect, absolute, a despotic cause-and-effect chain. To isolate that moment as the cause of his death six months later is to ignore the circumstances that brought him to that juncture, as well as all the alternatives the intervening months offered. But Joe is a story-teller, and every story – in Hollywood, at least – is supposed to have a beginning, a middle and an end, even if *Sunset Blvd.* interferes with that order so that the end appears to be implicit in the beginning. The world of the film is determinist, but Joe's telling of it is fatalist. His resignation transforms his telling of the world into a cause-and-effect chain whose links, because they can be constructed and told in one direction, seem also to be tellable in reverse, producing a sense of inevitability. But links are forged: they are made, shaped, crafted. They are fabrications, the product of a telling. They have the logic of story, not of world.

D.O.A. is narrated not by a dead man but a dying one. Just as Frank seems to be propelled through police headquarters by the camera, so he is propelled through a narrative which, although at times confused and confusing, seems equally predetermined. As he races from location to location, bursting into room after room, his investigation folding back on itself, laying out possible permutations of characters and crimes until he hits on the right one, his path seems anything but predetermined. However, the narrative is not of his investigation but of his death, of the progress of the poison, of his body's failing resistance. In the film's later stages, the action accelerates as if Frank can hear his body counting down. The drive to the climax becomes desperate, hastily tying all the ends together. As long as he keeps talking, he cannot die; but he must talk quickly to tell his story before he dies.

Detour's Al is a tale-teller, too, but with a less certain linguistic facility. As a hitchhiker, he can never tell whether he is talking too much or too little.

FIGURE 5 Dead man walking: *D.O.A.*

He responds to Haskell's sexist tirade with cautiously grunted affirmatives. He loses every argument with Vera. He becomes tongue-tied when trying to sell Haskell's car. But there is a contradiction between the tale Al tells and the telling of that tale. His voice-over reveals a deadpan hard-boiled – if self-pitying and self-serving – fluency and wit: 'While the mechanic inspected the car, we haggled. At last, when we were all worn out, we reached a compromise. His price.'

Al's recollection of the past is 'in itself a means of blotting it out, and his commentary, far from serving as the clue which leads us infallibly to the meaning of the narrative action, is like a palimpsest beneath which we may glimpse the traces of the history he has felt compelled to rewrite' (Britton 1992: 175). In the contradictions in the voice-over and between it and depicted events, Andrew Britton finds 'the residue of the process of rationalisation and revision to which all Al's memories have been subjected' (1992: 177). For example, his explanation of why he took Haskell's identity sounds like the rehearsal of post-hoc justification:

I saw at once he was dead and I was in for it. Who would believe he fell out of the car? Why, if Haskell came to, which of course he couldn't, even he would swear I'd conked him over the head for his dough. Yes, I was in for it. Instinct told me to run, but then I realised it was hopeless. There were lots of people back down the road who could identify me. That gas station guy and the waitress. I'd be in a worse spot then, trying to explain why I beat it. The next possibility was to sit tight and tell the truth when the cops came, but that would be crazy. They'd laugh at the truth, and I'd have my head in a noose. So what else was there to do than hide the body and get away in the car?

In narrativising himself, Al constructs a victim of circumstances, guilty only of accepting a lift one day in Arizona: 'Until then I'd done things my way, but from then on something else stepped in and shunted me off to a different destination from the one I had picked for myself.' This self-construction is not merely verbal: the camera which tracks in on Al's perpetually hangdog

FIGURE 6 Perpetually hangdog: *Detour*

face in the frame-story diner seems, in his flashback, to prowl through the night-club, hunting for him.

Detour's opening shot, although not connected to the narrative, is suggestive: it is a retrospective view. When we first encounter Al, he is heading from west to east, not only rescinding his previous journey but also the trajectory of western mythology. When heading west (to Hollywood, where his fiancée awaits him) and into the future, Al seeks some vaguely-defined goal, never looking back (to see, as we do in the opening shot, a broken-down car beside a desert road). He lurches from situation to situation, thinking he is making progress, even though the west coast, where Sue has been reduced to hash-slinging, can offer no solution to their impoverishment. Turned around, and heading back east, he can see only catastrophe. Short on self-knowledge and lacking even Vera's critical acumen – she has few illusions about the workings of capitalism and patriarchy – he can only make sense of himself as someone who has been randomly and unjustly victimised: 'Yes, fate or some mysterious force can put the finger on you or me for no good reason at all.' This obvious resort to a metaphysical agency to excuse his actions points to an ideological obfuscation in which individual agency is treated as an isolatable single cause, as if it were consciousness that determined social existence rather than social existence that determined consciousness. The mystificatory reduction of agency to individual psychology obscures the extent to which that psychology and agency, understood as causes, are also, perhaps primarily, effects. Where Joe's voice-over is addressed directly to the audience and Frank's to a surrogate audience, Al's is addressed primarily to himself – a self-justification and the rehearsal of a confession which we overhear. This emphasises the extent of Al's alienation. Talking to himself he can control language and master himself, albeit through misrecognising himself in the narrative subject he constructs; but plunged into an intersubjective arena, he comes adrift, stumbling over both words and roads. As Al's words and the narrative they shape come to an end, so does his aimless easterly wandering. Stopped by the police, he is silent; with nothing left to say, he is arrested.

While each of these three films posits a determinist universe, the combination flashback/voice-over foregrounds the process of narrative construction by which determinism becomes confused with notions of cause-and-effect, predictability and inevitability. Determinism is better imagined in terms of a continually collapsing wavefront simultaneous with rather than anterior to the moment. Cause-and-effect is a retrospectively-constructed trajectory through this succession of simultaneities. Emerging from a narrativising impulse, cause-and-effect produces (illusory) inevitability-effects and fuels the mistaking of determinism for predictability. Its telling is partial.

As Britton notes, the American road is typically mythologised as a site of 'individual resistance to the constraints of an intolerably oppressive, conservative and regimented culture', but *Detour* insists on reconnecting the individual with social institutions, reimagining the road not as 'a refuge for exiles from a culture in which American ideals have been degraded, but [as] a place where the logic of advanced capitalist civil society is acted out by characters who have completely internalised its values, and whose interaction exemplifies the grotesque deformation of all human relationships by the principles of the market' (1992: 182). Although not all film noirs are as explicit in their social critique as *Detour*, many combine depictions of rationalised or mechanistic processes with potent images of determinate discourses and social structures.

Although few would now argue that film noir shattered the dominant imagistic conventions of classical Hollywood, the overt and excessive stylisation of *Stranger on the Third Floor*'s six-and-a-half-minute dream-sequence pushes very hard against them. Joe Briggs (Elisha Cook, Jr) is convicted of a brutal murder on circumstantial evidence and the testimony of struggling journalist Mike Ward (John McGuire), who discovered him standing over the corpse. Mike's fiancée, Jane (Margaret Tallichet), is not convinced of Briggs's guilt, and Mike himself begins to entertain doubts. He chases a mysterious stranger (Peter Lorre) from his apartment building. When Mike cannot hear the snoring of his interfering neighbour, Albert Meng (Charles Halton), he imagines that Meng is dead. Mike realises that his own past behaviour and angry words would provide exactly the kind of circumstantial evidence that convicted Briggs. He falls asleep and enters a nightmare world of exaggerated proportions, distorted perspectives and barren minimalist sets which emphasise his isolation and incarceration. He wakes up and finds Meng has indeed been butchered, just like Briggs' supposed victim. No-one believes Mike's story of the stranger, but Jane eventually finds the mentally-unbalanced killer, who dies after confessing to the murders.

Mike's dream, often cited as evidence of German Expressionism's influence on film noir, merely hystericises the primary diegesis, itself a remarkable world of dark shadows and pools of light in which the courtroom statue of Justice becomes ominous, as if her blindfold does not promise impartiality but signals an inability to see clearly. The dream sequence's anti-realist distortions might well derive from *Das Kabinet des Dr. Caligari*, but film noir worlds resemble *Stranger on the Third Floor*'s waking world, and not just visually. It foregrounds the economics of everyday life – Mike's enthusiasm for testifying is linked to a payrise which will finally enable him to marry Jane – as well as the sexual repressiveness and libidinal underbelly of conventional morality; and it is in the waking world that Mike unwittingly describes the extent of his entrapment, protesting to the D.A., 'I'm as sane as you are, and if you think I had anything to do with it, you're crazy'.

A claustrophobic *mise-en-scène* composed of encroaching darkness and visual distortions was common to film noirs, often for economic reasons because in autumn 1942 'the war Production Board imposed a ceiling of $5,000 on new materials for set construction, and ways of economising included using lighting techniques which minimise the limitations of the sets' (Walker 1992a: 27). The techniques developed to deal with these restrictions would later be important to the independent production companies that proliferated after the 1948 Paramount decision, but not all film noirs relied upon them to create a sense of entrapment. Although its sets are not as minimalist as *Detour*'s, Lang's *Beyond a Reasonable Doubt* is extremely pared down, with a flat visual style and relentless narrative. Ex-newspaperman and would-be novelist Tom Garrett (Dana Andrews), plots with his former boss, Austin Spencer (Sidney Blackmer), who is also the father of his fiancée, Susan (Joan Fontaine), to be wrongly convicted for murder so as to discredit capital punishment. Having planted evidence and positioned himself as a suspect, Tom is soon given the death penalty, but the evidence of his innocence is destroyed when Austin is killed on his way to expose the erroneous conviction. Just before Tom is to be executed, an account of their plan is found among Austin's papers. When Susan tells Tom of his imminent pardon, he accidentally reveals that he *is* guilty of the murder and confesses to using Austin's scheme to get away with it. Susan intervenes before the pardon can be signed and Tom is returned to death row. Douglas Pye identifies several narrative, rather than visual, techniques which draw the viewer through this remorselessly unfolding narrative. Because we know about Austin's plan from the outset, we 'are therefore likely to believe that we have privileged access to narrative information'

(1992: 104). Each of the film's forty sequences are closely linked to those which precede and follow it, producing 'a sense of very strong narrative progression' (ibid.); this is accelerated by omitting transitional shots and only showing each scene's narrative kernel. Characters are rarely seen in isolation, depriving us of insights into their thoughts and feelings. The camera is generally distanced from characters, discouraging our participation and 'requir[ing] us to scrutinise the characters' (1992: 106) rather than empathise with them. The actors' performances are muted, too. Where *Detour*'s Al, disguised as Haskell, melodramatically refers to 'this nightmare of being a dead man', *Beyond a Reasonable Doubt* is populated with automata, people subjected to rationalised, if absurd, processes. Both Austin's and Tom's schemes are every bit as instrumentalist as the death penalty Austin wishes to discredit.

While *Detour* refers back to the Depression, *Pitfall* firmly locates its critique in the postwar world, introducing concerns which would become far more prominent in Eisenhower's placid decade. The opening sequence, in which insurance agent John Forbes (Dick Powell) breakfasts with his wife, Sue (Jane Wyatt), and son, Tommy (Jimmy Hunt), focuses on his dissatisfaction with his comfortable life. Married to his high-school sweetheart, with whom he once dreamed of sailing around the world, he feels trapped by the responsibility of providing for his family, by the interwoven determinants of capitalism and patriarchy structuring his social being. He does not want to be just one of fifty million average Americans, and longs for an idealised exotic Latin America of, in Sue's words, 'dusky dames'. His one-night stand with model Mona Stevens (Lizabeth Scott) is unsurprising, then, but despite initial appearances she is no femme fatale. When she discovers Forbes is married, she refuses further romantic or sexual involvement. This interest in female identity, however much the unfolding thriller narrative might marginalise it, has been signalled before Mona's appearance. Dropping John off at work, Sue points out that she too is getting bored with his routine farewell peck on the cheek. He kisses her on the mouth, but as he turns to get out of the car he misses the less-than-impressed expression that indicates her own sexual dissatisfaction.

Caught opens with carhop Maud (Barbara Bel Geddes) and her roommate Maxine (Ruth Brady) leafing through a fashion magazine, admiring jewels and furs, while the *mise-en-scène* reveals the gulf between current situation and idealised lifestyle. While Maud bathes her aching feet, Maxine questions her about day-to-day expenses. As she calculates how long it will take Maud to save up for a night-school course, the limited choices available to these women become clear: the course is at the Dorothy Dale School of Charm, where Maud will learn elocution and comportment in order to become a department-store model like Maxine in the vague hope that she will meet a 'real man' – defined, by Maxine, as someone able to buy her a fur coat (later, explicit parallels are drawn between modelling and prostitution). Maud, who changes her name to Leonora, *does* meet and marry a wealthy man, tycoon Smith Ohlrig (Robert Ryan). A montage sequence perfectly captures her entrapment within a conflation of capitalism, patriarchy and the American dream, with newspaper headlines equating her transformation from a carhop to Mrs Ohlrig with success, as if marrying into wealth is the pinnacle of female ambition and achievement. Unknown to Leonora, however, Smith married her in a fit of pique when a psychiatrist diagnosed his heart problems as psychosomatic responses to not getting his own way. A tyrannical husband, he neglects Leonora, treating her like an employee. Shot composition and *mise-en-scène* dwarf her, and depth of field frequently emphasises the emotional distance between the unhappy couple.

The resolution is deeply problematic. Leonara becomes a receptionist and falls in love with one of her employers, paediatrician Dr Larry Quinada (James Mason), who despite his wealthy background has chosen to work among New York's impoverished. However, the happy ending depends upon Leonora, pregnant by Ohlrig but in love with Quinada, giving premature birth to a child who dies. The Cinderella story of romantic love and social advancement is replaced by one of romantic love, noble self-sacrifice and suffering, but both are refuted. If the 'ideological significance of lovers living happily ever after lies in the unspoken, and usually invisible, metamorphosis that is implied to take place at the end of every happy ending [by which] lovers are transformed into mothers and fathers, into families' (Harvey 1998: 37), this resolution is disturbed in *Caught* by the infant's unseen corpse, a material remnant blocking ideological closure.

Beyond the Forest is similarly structured around the triangular relationship between a woman who desires wealth, a callous millionaire and a self-sacrificing doctor; an unwanted pregnancy precipitates its final crisis, too. However, the protagonist, Rosa Moline (Bette Davis), is a femme fatale – or, rather she would be if the film was told from the perspective of one of the male characters. A gold-digger whose ascent has stalled, her flashback narrative humanises her, preventing her reduction to a seductive image. This emphasis on the sexual woman as a character is not the only change worked on familiar film noir patterns; it also reworks the city/country dichotomy which shapes noir geography. While *The Big Heat* and Siodmak's *The Killers* contrast the noir city with exurban domestic idylls (one is outside the city, in the suburbs, the other above the city, on the roof), so *Out of the Past* and *On Dangerous Ground* (1952) contrast the noir city with a redemptive countryside. This opposition is ironised by the artifice of *You Only Live Once*'s honeymoon lodge where the couple-on-the-run try to romanticise a pond full of croaking frogs and of *Gun Crazy*'s montage of back-projected 'postcard' images in front of which the couple-on-the-run try to go straight; and by *The Asphalt Jungle*'s Dix Handley (Sterling Hayden), who commits crimes to buy back the family farm, only to die of a gunshot wound when, on the run, he finally reaches it. *Beyond the Forest* offers a more complex revision of these terms and the values they represent.

For Rosa, Loyalton is a prison, overseen by an infernal mill that 'sucks all the juice out of' it and populated with small-minded, unambitious, mundane people, resigned to or, more damningly, contented with their lot. Rosa longs for material goods and big city life, but her husband Lewis (Joseph Cotten), likes being a small-town doctor, despite persistent financial difficulties. He relishes being part of a community, while Rosa, ever since she was a schoolgirl, has sought to set herself apart, desired to be something other than a wife and mother. Rather than trying to make her way in the city as a young single woman, she strategically married Lewis, thus obtaining a sense of upward mobility. Further advancement has been thwarted by Lewis's contrary ambition to be a good small-town general practitioner rather than a big-city specialist. The flashback narrative – Rosa is on trial for murder – opens with Rosa, Lewis and Moose (Minor Watson), a recovering alcoholic, making their way to a hunting lodge in the mountains. Once there, manipulative Rose sends Lewis back to Loyalton and gets Moose drunk. She then waits in the neighbouring lodge for her lover, millionaire Neil Latimer (David Brian), who laughs at her suggestion that she should divorce Lewis and marry him.

Increasingly discontented with her home and marriage – 'If I don't get out of here, I'll die; if I don't get out of here, I hope I die' – Rosa demands that Lewis's patients pay their bills. She uses the money to visit Latimer in

Chicago, where he tells her he is in love with another woman. Lewis made it clear that if she went she should not come back, but on her return, as a later plot twist implies, she uses sex to change his mind. Latimer, realising that really he wants Rosa, returns. When Moose threatens to tell Latimer of her pregnancy by Lewis, Rosa 'accidentally' shoots him while hunting. Because no one knows of the affair, Rosa does not appear to have a motive for killing Moose. She is acquitted, but Latimer now wants to postpone their plans so there will not be any scandal. Fearful that Latimer will not marry her if he knows she is pregnant, she tells Lewis everything. He tells her she can go anywhere and do whatever she pleases – after she has had his baby. She throws herself down a mountainside to induce a miscarriage, to get rid of the 'dirt hanging to' her. Delirious, desperately ill and convinced that Lewis is poisoning her, she makes her escape, only to die before she can reach the train station.

Throughout the film, the domestic is never idyllic, but the site of a clash of wills between Rosa, who has very clear ideas about housework (which is beneath her), and her slovenly, idle and, above all, reluctant maid. Nor is the surrounding countryside idyllic for Rosa. It might be beautiful, and even restful for Lewis, but it is also the site of adultery and murder, not redemption. On the first trip to the lodge, Rosa's high-heels signal not only her incongruous presence but also her instrumentalism: she is there to seduce Latimer. The hoe-down to celebrate Moose's birthday and the return of his estranged daughter might evoke an image of community familiar from John Ford's westerns, but it is criss-crossed by the sexual tensions that result in Moose's death the following morning. Similarly, the city is positioned between two sets of associations, alternating throughout the Chicago sequence as a place of hope for Rosa, then of despair as she cannot contact Latimer, then of hope again when he arranges to meet her. Finally, when he has told her of his plans to marry someone else, the city becomes noirishly distorted, disorientating and threatening as she runs off into the rain.

A number of film noirs, including *The Fallen Sparrow*, *Cornered* (1945), *The Blue Dahlia*, *Crack-Up*, *Somewhere in the Night* (1946), *Dead Reckoning* (1947), *Ride the Pink Horse* (1947) and *The Crooked Way* (1949), focus on returning war veterans who are often physically, mentally or emotionally traumatised. Like *I Am a Fugitive from a Chain Gang*, these films often transform the disorientation of return to society into a sense that society itself is disoriented. As Harvey suggests:

the encounter with a depressed peacetime economy, with its threat of high prices and rising unemployment, began a process of general disillusionment for many of those returning home after the war, in search of the values which they had fought to defend. It is this breakdown also, this erosion of expectations, that finds its way into film noir by a series of complex transmutations. The hard facts of economic life are transmuted ... into corresponding moods and feelings. Thus the feelings of loss and alienation expressed by the characters in film noir can be seen as the product both of post-war depression and of the reorganisation of the American economy. (1998: 39)

Although focused on film noir's returning (white) veterans, this argument also contextualises the situation of *Caught*'s Maud/Leonora and Mildred (Joan Crawford) in *Mildred Pierce* (1945). While *Shadow of a Doubt, Beware, My Lovely* and *On Dangerous Ground* might be regarded as metaphoric treatments of loved ones coming to terms with war-traumatised men, *The Reckless Moment* focuses instead on the wife who was left behind to raise the family. Lucia Harper (Joan Bennett) lives in the wealthy Californian community of Balboa with her father and her two teenage children, Bea (Geraldine Brooks) and David (David Bair). Her husband, who is away on business, is despatched by his company to Berlin to help rebuild a bridge. Unable to return home for Christmas before going overseas, he is absent throughout. Lucia, who coped without him for three years during the war, does not shrink from confronting sordid Ted Darby (Shepperd Strudwick), who has been dating Bea, nor from disposing of his corpse after his acci-dental death. However, Bea's incautious love-letters have fallen into the hands of Nagle (Roy Roberts), and his associate, Martin Donnelly (James Mason), who want $5,000 for them. The shadows in Lucia's house seem to coalesce around soft-spoken Donnelly's dark presence, but as he spends time with her, the brooding blackmailer, seeing how she is surrounded by a family from which she can never escape, feels a growing sympathy for her. Unable to contact her husband, she cannot borrow money from her bank or a loan company. In a touching moment, having struggled to find the money by planning future household economies, she briefly, half-heartedly, com-plains about the amount of electricity her family wastes by never switching off the lights. In his penultimate scene with Lucia, Donnelly tells her about his childhood. One of five sons, his mother, who could never see that he was the bad one, wanted him to become a priest: 'I never did a decent thing in all my life. I never even wanted to until you came along. Then I began to think if only I could turn back and start over. So what happens? As soon as I try to start back I find myself with this on my hands.' At the end of the film, Mr Harper phones from Germany. As Lucia takes the phone, the camera entraps her behind the banister as her family surround her. Donnelly might have yearned for Lucia and for family life, and have been prepared to die so as to preserve Lucia's family, but this final shot indicates that Lucia is every bit the prisoner he had earlier suggested – even if she does not realise it.

Throughout, the film has toyed with the audience. When Lucia returns from dumping Darby's corpse, she is told she should not have taken the boat out as it needs new spark plugs: one breathes a sigh of relief. Lucia and Donnelly appear together in potentially compromising situations: will people think that she is having an affair? Much is made of Lucia's mis-placed shopping list: will it be found with Darby's corpse? At these and other junctures, the narrative could have gone in very different directions. That it does not might seem to confirm Donnelly's fatalism; but again, the narrative is just one route through the branching possibilities at which the film hints. One does not have to reject determinism to deny the inevitability of this particular series of events. Rather, the alternatives routes the narra-tive might take exist precisely because of the nest of determining frames from which the actual narrative emerges. It is how the wavefront collapses but, as the alternative possibilities suggest, there is no compelling reason for it to have collapsed into this particular trajectory.

On some level, narratives are always about the possibility of agency, as the comparison of *La Bête humaine* and *Double Indemnity* demonstrated. After the Second World War, as the collectivism represented by the New Deal Administration and fighting the war mutated into the Cold War con-sensus, as postwar capitalism demanded the replacement of the heroic entrepreneurial individual with the organisation man (and ambition, drive and initiative with personality and fitting-in), so America increasingly took on the image of the reified commodity universe described by the Frankfurt School. This dominant instrumentalism was exemplified by the postwar accommodation between labour and capital (see Davis 1986) – or, rather, the negotiated subordination of labour to capital – and the constraints it imposed on the social realm shape the film noir world in which individuals struggle for agency, for being. The protagonists discussed in this section are ultimately trapped by having to sell their labour in a world which does not necessarily want or need to buy it but denies alternative modes of existence. They are webbed into social and institutional relations which are dominated by exchange value and egotistical calculation and which deny them egress. Mostly, they are guilty of just wanting to pay the bills, or of wanting a break from the relentless necessity of doing so.

Investigation

From *Stranger on the Third Floor* to *The Naked Kiss*, the investigation was a staple film noir plot, albeit often obscured, distorted, derailed. While the underlying logic of this plot is that the world can be known, the film noir investigator frequently struggles to reconstruct and tell an order of events that make any kind of sense. Coincidences, hidden interrelations, unclear and confused motives abound. Consequently, the film noir investigator repeatedly uncovers the order embedded deep within chaos, witnesses order emerging from chaos; he or she then, typically, has to construct plausible cause-and-effect chains to tell what has happened, to map a particular – and partial – trajectory. In doing so, the film noir investigator offers a model of the complexly-determined 'fuzzy' subject (see Bould 2002). This section will focus in particular on the linguistic determination of the masculine subject in six investigative and two heist film noirs. It will begin, however, with a consideration of hard-boiled prose.

According to Frank Krutnik, 1940s Hollywood turned to hard-boiled crime fiction for two related reasons. With many leading writers, directors and stars drafted, and with externally-imposed budgetary restrictions, the studios needed 'alternative production values', such as 'story source' (1991: 37), with which to appeal to audiences. Wartime paper-rationing meant less fiction was being published, so they turned to pre-war pulps like *Black Mask* and their professional writers, who were used to producing serviceable prose to deadlines.

In *Murder, My Sweet* patrician con-man Amthor (Otto Kruger) criticises Marlowe's 'unpleasant tendency toward abrupt transitions, a characteristic of your generation' – an observation equally applicable to 'the *Black Mask* type of story', in which 'the scene outranked the plot in the sense that a good plot was one which made good scenes' (Chandler 1980: 10). (This description of plot strongly resonates with the notion of cause-and-effect as a partial and retrospective telling of a trajectory abstracted from a total system which changes from moment to moment.) Chandler continues:

> We who tried to write it had the same point of view as the film-makers. When I first went to Hollywood a very intelligent producer told me that you couldn't make a successful motion picture from a mystery story, because the whole point was a disclosure that took a few seconds of screen time while the audience was reaching for its hat. He was wrong, but only because he was thinking of the wrong kind of mystery ... Undoubtedly the [hard-boiled] stories ... had a fantastic element. Such things happened, but not so rapidly, nor to so close-knit a group of people, nor within so narrow a frame of logic. This was inevitable because the demand was for constant action; if you stopped to think you were lost. When in doubt, have a man come through a door with a gun in his hand. (Ibid.)

This match between hard-boiled fiction and film noir is demonstrated by the frequency with which a man with a gun, or some equivalent, does indeed walk in through the door. The flashback narrative of *Murder, My Sweet* begins with Marlowe, bored and restless. As he sits in his office, waiting for his date to phone, Moose Malloy suddenly appears, a giant figure reflected in Marlowe's window. Despite his bulk, his approach has been noise-less. He makes other equally sudden appearances: at the night club; after Marlowe's escape from the clinic where he has been held a prisoner; at Marlowe's office again. Such abrupt entrances, and the narrative twists and turns that follow, are not limited to adaptations of Chandler. *D.O.A.* shuffles and reshuffles its characters in this way. *Caught* dangles potential narrative forks. In *Pitfall*, psychotic thug MacDonald (Raymond Burr) exists mainly to perform tasks equivalent to walking through the door with a gun.

William Marling (1995) suggests intriguing parallels between hard-boiled fiction and the transition in 1920s design from organic, static, detailed Victoriana to streamlined, smooth, dynamic moderne. The overall trajectory suggested by the careful ordering of a series of components – exemplified by the episodic and telegraphic verticality of the stepback skyscraper – is homologous to the narrative form Chandler ascribes to hard-boiled fiction and of investigative film noirs. The privileging of scene over plot is evident in the famous anecdote about *The Big Sleep* in which Bogart, baffled by the labyrinthine plot, asked who had actually killed one of the characters. Neither director Howard Hawks nor screenwriters Jules Furthman, William Faulkner and Leigh Brackett knew, so they asked Chandler, who did not know either. Furthermore, as David Thomson suggests, a number of characters – the Acme bookshop proprietress (Dorothy Malone), Harry Jones (Elisha Cook, Jr), Joe Brody (Louis Jean Heydt), Agnes (Sonia Darrin) – are superfluous to the film, prompting his claim that *The Big Sleep* 'is one of the most formally radical pictures ever made in Hollywood ... a kind of ongoing rehearsal or improvisation ... a celebration of acting, dialogue (as opposed to talk) and fantasising' (1997: 64). Such hyperbole stems from over-attendance to conventional notions of classical Hollywood narrative – notions which, while recognising the importance of spectacular spectacle (song-and-dance routines, fistfights, gunfights, landscapes, chases, physical routines), consistently underplay the importance of the non-spectacular spectacle (the romantic embrace, melodrama's suffering, science fiction's pseudo-scientific chatter and, most importantly, across all genres, the spectacle of stars delivering dialogue) and the way such attractions are often privileged over a coherent narrative arc. While *The Big Sleep* might be remarkable, it is far from exceptional. With budgetary restrictions on more overt material spectacle, sensuous pleasure in dialogue is precisely one of the alternative production values Hollywood could utilise; and, as Krutnik notes,

> one of the defining features of 'hard-boiled' writing is its language. The 'hard-boiled' idiom is 'tough', cynical, epigrammatic, controlled – a sign of the hero's potency ... In many of the private-eye stories, language is wielded as a weapon, and is often more a measure of the hero's prowess than the use of guns and other more tangible aids to violence. Confrontations between the hero and his adversaries frequently take the form of extended sessions of verbal sparring as each seeks to assert his masculine competence. There may occasionally be 'wise-cracking' dames, but this often signifies a dangerous competitive streak ... More often, the books set up an opposition between the male as language user and the woman as erotic object, as a glorified body of awesome excitation (which poses its own dangers, of overwhelming male rationality). (1991: 43)

This is evident even in an author as crude as Carroll John Daly. In 'Three Gun Terry' (1923), 'the first tough detective story starring the world's first wisecracking, hard-boiled private investigator' (Nolan 1985: 43), there is no dame, merely an innocent – and nearly voiceless – girl, defined almost exclusively in terms of her physicality and the reactions she prompts in phallic Terry whose coherence is constantly threatened by her:

> Say, but that girl was scared; why, she didn't do nothing but hang close to me and keep her head up against my chest as she clung to my coat. And she was mighty little and mighty young too, I think, though I couldn't tell much about her, there in the dark of the cab. Somehow I felt almost like a father as I patted her little dark head and ran my fingers through her soft black locks. I could 'a laughed, but somehow I didn't ... And there I was, telling her that she was all right, and that I'd take care of her and – and – oh – just acting like a regular nut. What I should 'a been doing was questioning her and finding out just what her old man was worth and how much there would be in it for me. But somehow I didn't do anything but try to comfort her like she was a baby.
> [...]
> And in about five minutes she comes in, and she's a wow. I didn't get a good look at her before, and I tell you it's a lucky thing I ain't romantic ... Even me, a hardened citizen like me – yep, I was nearly ready to take ten dollars off the bill...
> [...]
> And right there is another thing that I can't explain. Maybe it's weakness, but I like to think it ain't, though I can't account for it. You might think that I had done enough for this girl and earned my pay – well, perhaps I had. But there was soft little hands around my neck and silken hair against my cheek – great innocent, childish eyes looking through pools of water into mine – and – well, I stayed – yep, I just played the fool and stayed.
>
> So it was I held her in my arms when half a dozen cops busted into the room. (Daly 1985: 46, 50, 67)

This is not to claim that there was a single hard-boiled voice – compare Hammett's 'objective' prose, resolutely external to characters, leaving their motives to be interpreted from their closely observed actions, with Woolrich's baroque, almost-out-of-control contortions – nor that all film noirs sought to replicate hard-boiled dialogue.

The latter point can be observed by comparing *Murder, My Sweet* to *Crossfire* (1947), made three years apart by the same producer (Adrian Scott), director (Edward Dmytryk) and screenwriter (John Paxton). Both are adapted from novels, respectively Chandler's *Farewell, My Lovely* and Richard Brooks's *The Brick Foxhole* (1945), the former a hard-boiled classic, the latter a more self-consciously literary fiction. The narrative structure of each novel was altered. *Murder, My Sweet* excised plot complications and changed the climax, while *Crossfire* substantially reworked its source, not only to remove material about homosexuality and homophobia (see Corber 1997, Naremore 1998) – emphasising instead the novel's condemnation of racism in general and anti-Semitism in particular – but to provide a structure more appropriate to a noir crime-investigation. While little dialogue is retained from either source, these sources do seem to dominate Paxton's dialogue. *Murder, My Sweet* is full of wisecracks, tough-guy slang and recurring bird and animal imagery. *Crossfire*'s more measured dialogue is virtually free of such ornamentation. This can be seen in the contrast between Marlowe's quips – 'I gave her a drink. She was a gal who would take a drink if she had to knock you down to get the bottle' – and the weary resignation of *Crossfire*'s brilliantly underplayed Detective Finlay (Robert Young). (The lack of linguistic ornamentation might also arise from *Crossfire*'s generic affiliation with the social problem film, as if its subject was too serious for pulp dialogue.) But, in different ways, both films privilege language. *Murder, My Sweet* relishes the textures of its idiom, whereas *Crossfire* depends upon several long dialogue scenes. With most of its $500,000 budget spent '*above* the line' on a cast which also included Robert Mitchum, Robert Ryan, Gloria Grahame, Sam Levene and Paul Kelly, that 'meant B picture expenditure *below* the line and a schedule of only twenty-two days' (Dmytryk 1996: 31). These constraints can be seen in the barrenness of sets (especially the hotel room, the waiting room and the cinema) as well as the duration of several scenes. Although the dialogue's unornamented texture might not suggest that it be considered an 'alternative production value', the film does rely upon the unspectacular spectacle of stars delivering dialogue.

Whatever its relationship with hard-boiled fiction, film noir should not be seen as a mere transcription from one medium to another. Film noir did produce distinctive effects, and one of the most important of these – the destabilisation of masculine authority – can be traced through the auto-critique of hard-boiled language increasingly evident in investigative film noirs.

Deborah Thomas identifies four characteristics shared by many film noirs. First, a 'central male protagonist whose point of view is privileged through such devices as first-person narration ... and subjective framing devices like flashbacks or dreams' (1992: 67). Second, an 'undermining of this point of view', either 'through labyrinthine plots which seem to elude the protagonist's attempts to give them coherence through his narration' or through 'breaks in the protagonist's consciousness' (1992: 68). Third, a protagonist lacking self-knowledge and divided against himself; this is often projected onto his desire for and fear of both the femme fatale and the domesticated woman. Fourth, a 'mood of pervasive anxiety' which might be resolved by various means, including the death of the femme fatale and the 'imminent domesticity [which] may beckon just the other side of the film's final frame' (ibid.). Closely matching this pattern, *Murder, My Sweet* signals a significant variation on such investigative film noirs as *The Maltese Falcon* and *The Big Sleep*. *The Maltese Falcon* devotes considerable energy to con-stituting Sam Spade (Humphrey Bogart) as 'an ideal ego' (Krutnik 1991: 93), mastering those around him through linguistic manipulation and physical violence as well as through his possession of the point-of-view shot. In *The Big Sleep*, only the similarly-constituted Philip Marlowe (Humphrey Bogart) can draw together the many complex, incoherent plot threads into a resolu-tion. Such control eludes Dick Powell's Marlowe in *Murder, My Sweet*.

Murder, My Sweet opens with a view down onto a pool of light in the middle of a table around which sit Marlowe and his police interrogators. 'I remember you as a pretty noisy little fellow, son. All of a sudden you get quiet,' says one cop. 'You lost your book of answers?' asks another, 'Or are you just waiting for your lawyer?' These opening lines establish the film's concern with language as a means of intersubjective conflict and subject-constitution. The first cop implies his superiority by constructing the past from his perspective ('I remember'), subordinating an infantilised Marlowe ('a pretty noisy little fellow') and identifying himself with patriarchal author-ity ('son'). Marlowe's silence – his missing book of answers – cuts him off from the symbolic realm (a lawyer is, of course, a mouthpiece). Our first clear view of Marlowe's face, with a dressing covering his eyes, seems to complete this symbolic castration. Temporarily blinded, he is a private eye who cannot see. However, even from his disempowered position, he can talk; and so he tells how he came to this juncture, reconstituting his self, his history and his identity. With an official scribe recording his words, he speaks himself back into the symbolic realm and attempts to reduce this complexly-determined moment to the outcome of a clear cause-and-effect chain.

Marlowe often relies upon language to get his way. When Moose hires Marlowe to help find his ex-girlfriend, Velma, Marlowe asks how he can contact him – 'I contact you', Moose replies. When Lindsey Marriott (Douglas Walton) then tries to hire Marlowe without revealing too much about the job, Marlowe verbally bullies him, attempting, through self-possessed verbal aggression, to expunge his failure to subordinate Moose. Embodying a physical force linguistic skills cannot defeat and a materiality irreducible to language, the infantile Moose represents the return of repressed unconscious drives, the proletarian subject who cannot be suppressed by bourgeois subjectivity and the material kernel which refuses linguistic determination. His asserted authority is proleptic of the unmanning, the subjective disintegration, which Marlowe will undergo.

Marlowe accompanies Marriott to a nocturnal rendezvous, ostensibly to buy back a jade necklace belonging to Mr Grayle (Miles Mander) and stolen from Mrs Grayle (Claire Trevor), his second, younger, wife. Marlowe returns through the rising fog to find Marriott beaten to death. Clubbed from behind, Marlowe falls to the ground and his voice-over begins. 'I caught the blackjack right behind my ear. A black pool opened up at my feet. I dived right in. It had no bottom.' Blackness seeps across the screen until there is just a point of light at the centre. 'I felt pretty good. Like an amputated leg.' The point of light grows, irises out from Marlowe's face, which is held in a torch beam. As Marlowe struggles to his feet, the bearer of the torch flees. The pool imagery, which will reappear, is, like the film's vortical imagery, readily associated, as in *Vertigo*, with vaginal imagery and female identity. The 'amputated leg', like Jeffries' (James Stewart) broken leg in *Rear Window* (1954), alludes to castration. Beams of light often foreground the phallic gaze – as in Rotwang's torch-pursuit of Maria through *Metropolis*'s caverns; the spotlight in which the eponymous Gilda (Rita Hayworth) performs; and the torment by torchlight of Susan Vargas (Janet Leigh) in *Touch of Evil* (1958). But here, although it is not revealed until later, a woman

– Ann (Anne Shirley), Mr Grayle's daughter from his first marriage – wields the torch, further emasculating Marlowe.

When Marlowe reports Marriott's murder, he is warned against investigating it: 'All I want is your silence', Lieutenant Randall (Don Douglas) tells him. Marlowe, however, is then hired by the Grayles to recover the necklace, simultaneously and lasciviously appreciating both Mrs Grayle's appearance and the double meanings in her husband's discussion of his valuable pieces. When Mrs Grayle calls at Marlowe's apartment, he is standing in front of a mirror, brushing his hair. This narcissistic self-regard and the conversation that follows resonates strongly with the Lacanian mirror phase. In response to her questions, former cop Marlowe reveals that the D.A. fired him not for incompetence but for talking back, his Oedipal identification with legal, investigative and punitive authority shattered by insubordination, by a premature usurpation of language. In front of the mirror, he constructs himself both verbally and by dressing for their date. 'I had an interesting childhood, too,' he adds, before setting out for an expensive nightclub with Mrs Grayle, a sexualised mother figure (Grayle obviously puns on grail, a vaginal image that nonetheless emphasises patriarchal authority).

At the night-club, Mrs Grayle inexplicably disappears. Ann then attempts to hire Marlowe, but also disappears. Moose diverts Marlowe from his course by delivering him to Amthor, who confesses that this virtual kidnapping is an 'old psychological trick' to see what he might, off-balance, accidentally reveal. Their confrontation is a battle of linguistic registers, tones and vocabularies. Amthor is patrician and patronising, snobbish and effete, while Marlowe is earthier, colloquial and disrespectful. After chiding Marlowe for his 'abrupt transitions', Amthor insists that 'in this case, I must ask you to follow some sort of logical progression. Now, about the police?'. 'Either they've got something on you,' Marlowe replies, 'or they're trying to get it. I didn't expect you to tell me which. I was just baiting you. It's an old psychological trick, grandpa.' Marlowe seems confident that he has won this exchange – a conclusion one might dispute – but Amthor has already persuaded Moose that Marlowe knows Velma's whereabouts, and Marlowe is unable to convince him otherwise. The ensuing physical tussle ends with Amthor pistol-whipping Marlowe. As he falls to the ground, the camera loses focus and blackness again seeps across the screen, providing a particularly complex interplay of the discursive formations J. P. Telotte (1989) identifies. The third-person camera observing Marlowe is simultaneously conflated with Marlowe's fading consciousness and his retrospective description of losing consciousness, radically destabilising its authority.

Marlowe's subsequent dream is again full of vaginal imagery, phallic threats and a loss of control:

> The black pool opened at my feet again and I dived in. Next thing I remember was going somewhere. It was not my idea. [Two figures dump Marlowe on the floor.] The rest of it was a crazy cold-cut dream. [The image wavers.] I had never been there before. [Marlowe falls into space; giant heads quiz him; Moose reaches out for him; he falls again, into a swirling vortex. He is pursued through a series of doors hanging in dark empty space. Web-like threads drift across the image. He emerges through a too-small door. A giant doctor empties a giant syringe into him. He falls into another vortex. He wakes up beneath a bright light, the threads still obscuring his vision.] The window was open but the smoke did not move. It was a grey web woven by a thousand spiders. [He reaches out to the web.] I wondered how they got them to work together.

After a brief exchange with a male nurse and Moose, Marlowe settles back on his bed, rubbing his throat:

> My throat felt sore, but the fingers feeling it didn't feel anything. [He stretches out a hand toward the still-visible web.] They were just a bunch of bananas that looked like fingers. [He sits up.] I wondered what I was shot full of. Something to keep me quiet. Or something to make me talk. Maybe both. [He stands. The floor wobbles. He falls back onto the bed.] Okay, Marlowe, I said to myself, you're a tough guy. You've been sapped twice, choked, beaten silly with a gun, shot in the arm until you're as crazy as a couple of waltzing mice. [He begins to try to dress.] Now let's see you do something really tough, like putting your pants on. [He struggles to dress.] Okay, you cuckoo, walk and talk. What about? Anything, everything. Just talk and keep walking. [He staggers around the room.] You're getting out of here. That's a beautiful bed. Stay off it. Walk! I walked. I don't know how long. I didn't have a watch. They don't make that kind of time on watches anyway. [Finally, the web clears. He fastens his

cuffs. He is tidier but still dishevelled, his shirt sleeve badly torn.]
I was ready to talk to someone.

The divided subjectivity suggested by the earlier conflation of the camera with both narrator and narratee is here picked up by Marlowe as he recalls talking to himself, exerting linguistic control over his body and reconstituting himself out of language. Again, an essential part of this self-constitution is also effected by his costume. Throughout his walking-talking cure, his improving appearance matches his improving mental condition. Once his cuffs are fastened, he is ready not just to escape but to talk to someone else – but his torn sleeve signals if not incompleteness then certainly a chink in his armoured self.

Marlowe dips in and out of hysteria as he confronts Sonderborg (Ralf Harolde), the doctor who has been keeping him unconscious, and takes his gun. Sonderborg tries to persuade him he is sick and should return to bed. 'What were you saying?' Marlowe snaps. 'I made no remark,' Sonderborg replies. 'Remarks want you to make them,' says Marlowe. 'They've got their tongues out wanting to be said.' This Chandleresque phrasing suggests that language itself (rather than the speaking subject) has agency, that even the physical apparatus of speech (the punning 'tongues') belongs to language. Normally self-possessed, Marlowe feels this lack of agency mounting as the web returns to his field of vision. He wavers, but then banishes it by will alone. When Sonderborg equivocates, Marlowe points out, 'When you've got a gun in your hand, Doc, people are supposed to do what you tell them.' This phallic reassertion of self is reiterated as Marlowe forces Sonderborg to hand over a key – a symbol and instrument of his position – and then rips out the phone, depriving Sonderborg of his voice. Marlowe is far from secure, though. His own tongue betrays him when, on leaving the sanatorium, he stumbles into Moose and accidentally gives away vital information – but he has no idea what exactly it was that he should not have said. Moose, who usually merely overpowers him, here out-thinks him.

Marlowe accepts Grayle's offer to drop the case, intending to pursue it for his own reasons. He persuades Ann to hand over the beach house key: 'I could bust in, but a key would make it simpler.' Once inside, Marlowe admits to suspecting the motives behind her attentions. When she denounces him and all men, Mrs Grayle, who has been in hiding, overhears. Ann turns on her, decrying such 'big league blondes. Beautiful expensive babes who know what they've got. All bubble bath and dewy morning and moonlight. And, inside, blue steel. Cold, cold like that, only not that clean.' Ann storms out and Mrs Grayle sets about seducing Marlowe into her plan to dispose of Amthor, not knowing that Moose has already killed him. Marlowe, realising that she is Velda, arranges a confrontation with Moose for the following night. Unexpectedly, Grayle and Ann also turn up. The situation spirals out of Marlowe's control. Mrs Grayle is about to shoot him, when Grayle shoots her. Moose bursts in, finds the corpse and turns on Grayle. Marlowe tries to reach Grayle, but the gun goes off in front of his face.

In the interrogation room, Marlowe finishes his story. Blinded by the muzzle-flash, he lost consciousness. He heard three shots, but he does not know who was killed (Grayle and Moose died in the struggle over the gun). He keeps asking after Ann, who has been silently listening throughout the interrogation. She signals that they are not to reveal her presence and follows as Detective Nulty (Paul Phillips) escorts Marlowe from the building, all the time asking after Ann, expressing his feelings for her. When Marlowe is put in a cab, Ann takes Nulty's place. As they drive off, Marlowe recognises her but, pretending she is still Nulty, asks for a kiss. He removes his gun from his jacket, puts it aside, and the film closes with a romantic clinch.

The respective fates of Velda/Mrs Grayle and Ann recall the two responses to castration anxiety described by Laura Mulvey (1975). The sadistic-voyeuristic response identifies the guilty party and punishes her, while the fetishistic response substitutes a fetish object (Ann, who is infantilised as 'the kid' and made safe by her silence during the interrogation and departure from headquarters) for the dangerous female figure, the femme fatale – Ann's phallic ('inside, blue steel'), corrupt ('only not that clean'), too-young, and thus sexualised, stepmother.

Despite this, the end of the film is far from being a confident reassertion of masculinity and patriarchy. Marlowe's self-assertion gathers momentum as he effectively usurps Grayle, but the potential integration into the symbolic order signalled by Ann's partnership is undermined by his apparent preference for the sexualised mother. His attempted mastery dissolves when the cleverly-arranged confrontation ends with a woman pointing a gun at him and his symbolic castration. The police turn to Ann, doubly disempowered as a woman and 'the kid', to confirm his retrospective account, and even the conventional concluding formation of a heterosexual couple is undercut by its queer current. Homoeroticism bubbles up throughout the film (see Oliver and Trigo 2003), and this final swell evinces a tension central to patriarchal operations. Heterosexuality requires Marlowe to bond with Ann, whereas patriarchy requires him to identify with the masculine and homosocial law. Having disarmed himself, his voice, which has provided the spine of the film and his sense of self, is, courtesy of Ann's kiss, silenced.

If *Murder, My Sweet*'s attempt to replicate something of its source's first-person perspective was destabilised by its own cinematic techniques, then another Chandler adaptation, *Lady in the Lake*, pushed concern with technique to an extreme which shattered the stable identity of Chandler's Marlowe. With the exception of Marlowe's (Robert Montgomery) direct address to camera in the prologue, epilogue and an interpolated scene, the flashback narrative is told with a subjective camera which occupies Marlowe's position in each scene. On one level, Marlowe's challenge to the audience – 'You'll see it just as I saw it. You'll meet the people; you'll find the clues. And maybe you'll solve it quick, and maybe you won't' – is a neat avoidance of the problem of how to recount flashback events without subsequent knowledge distorting the account. It also represents an extension of the *Kammerspielfilm*'s experiment with the *enfesselte Kamera*, made possible by such wartime technological developments as 'the appearance of lightweight, mobile cameras like the German Arriflex and the introduction of the highly maneuvrable "crab" dolly that permitted longer takes [and] helped transform what previously was mainly a narrative punctuation, the subjective shot, into a viable narrative device' (Telotte 1989: 104). However, it also produces a sense of a simultaneously constrained and fragmented subject.

Despite attempts to humanise or, more accurately, masculinise and heterosexualise the subjective camera, as when Marlowe's distracted gaze turns from Adrienne Fromsett (Audrey Totter) to follow her secretary, one is left with a continual sense of disjunction. Although impressive, the camera replicates neither the human gaze ('its perspective and sense of dimension, among other things, are quite different' (Telotte 1989: 105)) nor human movement (purported eye-movements are too slow, 'more akin to movements of the head, complicated by a neckbrace' (Kawin 1978: 8)). Moreover, tracking and crane shots intended to suggest Marlowe's movement through his environment are too slow, as if the unchained camera is nonetheless hobbled.

This sense of constraint is exacerbated by two further factors. First, Telotte argues that the 45 shots which 'focus on entrances, depict characters using a door for access or egress, or employ doorways or windows to frame characters and create multiple planes of focus' create a sense of expectation, 'that there is always another door to enter, something new, unsuspected, and possibly threatening yet to be encountered', that 'simply opening a door can lead to various enigmas' (1989: 108–9). However, this proliferation of potential entrances and exits produces a slightly different effect, opening up the conflict between a complexly-determined total system and the impulse to narrate a particular cause-and-effect trajectory. Telotte describes the film's first subjective tracking shot, in which Marlowe's viewpoint wanders down a corridor, looking for the offices of Kingsby Publications, as 'the kind of shot that recurs in the film, repeatedly creating a maze-like effect, as the starting, then halting, camera signals an eye and a human presence, randomly moving and constantly opening onto the new and the unseen' (1989: 108). On the contrary, the retrospective telling and hobbled *enfesselte Kamera* suggests little that is random or unpremeditated: Marlowe knows he is going to Kingsby Publications, even if he must first find their office. In neo-formalist terms (see Bordwell 1985), the *fabula* (story) hints at alternatives while the *syuzhet* (plot) denies them. As one watches the film, the interaction of *fabula* and *syuzhet* produces, simultaneously, a sense of possibility and a sense of inevitability. Second, Montgomery's performance goes beyond the gruffness necessary to counter his image as a light romantic lead. His aggressiveness is evident in the prologue. Directly addressing the camera, he issues not an invitation to participate in the unravelling of the mystery but a crude, self-defensive challenge for the viewer to do any better than he did. He generally maintains this tone throughout, prompting confrontations and a similarly aggressive direct address from his interlocutors, who are usually held in fairly static medium shots. This combination of address and relative positioning fixes Marlowe in place, summoning back his wandering gaze, constraining him.

However, this direct address to Marlowe also passes straight through him to confront the discomfited viewer. Despite the omnipresence of his gaze, Marlowe lacks substance, his body is both fragmented (his hands never enter his field of vision from quite the right angle) and absent (his voice and footsteps sound curiously disembodied). When he sees his own reflection, his reflected body and the viewpoint never quite coincide and the latter remains static even when we can see his reflected head or eyes moving. This discrepancy between viewpoint and subject is most obvious when Chris Lavery (Richard Simmons) tricks Marlowe into looking at a mantelpiece clock in front of a large mirror. Lavery, reflected, is visible as he reaches for a knuckle-duster, but Marlowe is not.

Lavery knocks out Marlowe: his fist fills the screen, the viewpoint blurs, sways, falls to the ground, fades to black. Although narratively-motivated, this loss of consciousness is just one of several breaks in Marlowe's continuous subjectivity, the others being more conventionally-signalled omissions of transitional sequences. This failure to develop a subjective camera technique without recourse to the traditional grammar of cuts, fades and dissolves (as well as some very visible invisible cuts) has three distinct effects. First, it makes visible the constructedness of cause-and-effect while, second, distinguishing the cause-and-effect chain from the continuity of both consciousness and the total system. Third, it further fragments Marlowe, editing his consciousness and increasing his unreliability as a narrator (and author – he has turned, Hammett-like, from detective to pulp crime writer). This fragmentation is most pronounced by a pause in the narrative while Marlowe reappears as a direct-address narrator to tell of his trip to the morgue to view Muriel Chess's badly decomposed corpse. Despite Marlowe's opening challenge, the audience is denied the evidence of his (and its own) eyes. The private eye turned public, both as author and narrator/viewpoint, becomes private once more, denying the simultaneity of camera-subject and audience (upon which the film elsewhere insists) so as to mislead the audience. Instead of seeing through Marlowe's eyes, we hear a lie – Marlowe's misidentification of Crystal Kingsby's corpse, which he knows to be incorrect when he narrates it – and this sutures the viewer to a particular narrative trajectory just as Marlowe's error fixed his path through the potential maze represented (but never manifested) by all those other doors and windows.

Dark Passage also relies heavily, but less extensively, on a subjective camera. Vincent Parry (Humphrey Bogart), innocent of his wife's murder, escapes from San Quentin in order to find the killer. With the help of Irene Jansen (Lauren Bacall), whose father was similarly convicted – wrongly, according to Irene – of murdering his wife, Parry makes his way to San Francisco. A plastic surgeon alters his appearance, and it is only when the bandages are removed that we see Parry's – Bogart's – face. Hitherto, he has been represented primarily by prolonged subjective shots anchored by Bogart's voice. Although not always clear whether he is talking to himself or whether we are hearing his thoughts, this voice gives the audience some sense of Parry's interiority – a sharp contrast to Montgomery's abrasive loudmouth Marlowe. In addition to a more mobile camera, a greater use of the full depth of field and carefully underplayed performances by Parry's interlocutors (compare Totter's haranguing and visibly conniving Adrienne with Bacall's Irene, who glances, slides from beneath and exists outside of Parry's gaze), *Dark Passage* combines the subjective camera with conventional third-person camerawork. Consequently, the sutured-in Parry is part of the diegetic world in a way Montgomery's never-quite-present Marlowe is not.

Dark Passage does not, however, offer a secure image of masculine identity. In order to be free, Parry must surrender his face, name and identity and flee to Peru, but this surrender is also a consummation. Bogart's unmistakable voice makes Parry's own face, seen in newspaper photographs, seem like the fake one. The concluding scene sees not only Bogart's voice and face reunited, but also Parry and Irene, Bogart and Bacall – a simultaneous union of fictional, star and real-life couple. Moreover, Parry, seated in an exotic night-club, seems to have been made over as *Casablanca*'s (1942) Rick. These conflations are profoundly compensatory – as if the film knows it cannot resolve the questions of identity it prompts, and so shuts them down by transforming Parry into Bogart. (A similar play on Bogart's screen personas – as ruthless heavy and, later, romantic hero – constitutes Dix Steele, the screenwriter with the absurdly phallic name he plays in *In a Lonely Place*. Whereas Parry's voice provides continuity, writer-for-hire Dix is torn between attempting to maintain his own voice and an almost-incoherent rage. His romance with Laurel Gray (Gloria Grahame) comes to an end because the ruthless heavy erupts through the romantic hero, ironically confirming him as the latter.)

In several later film noirs, the fragmentation of the hero extends to the fragmentation of the diegetic world itself. For example, *Touch of Evil*'s extreme yet incoherent stylisations restlessly combine distorted compositions and unusual angles with abrupt shifts in tempo and, in its climatic scene, the dislocation, disembodiment and echoing reproduction of voices. *Kiss Me Deadly*, with its opening sequence's downward-scrolling titles and conspicuous manipulation of continuity errors and discrepancies between the volume and relative position of sound sources, introduces a similarly disconnected, discontinuous world. As in *Murder, My Sweet*, there is linguistic conflict between the pompous villain, Dr Soberin (Albert Dekker), who litters his speech with mythological allusions, and an inexpressive Mike Hammer (Ralph Meeker) who describes his violent propensities as being able 'to speak a lot of languages – any country you go to, you can take care of yourself'. There is also a strong sense of self-construction through external appearance. Resembling the armoured fascist male described by Klaus Theweleit (1987, 1989), Hammer is described by Christina (Cloris Leachman):

> You only have one real lasting love ... You. You're one of those self-indulgent males who thinks about nothing but his clothes, his car, himself. Bet you do push-ups every morning just to keep your belly hard ... I could tolerate flabby muscles in a man if it would make him more friendly. You're the kind of person who never gives in a relationship, who only takes. Ah, woman, the incomplete sex. What does she need to complete her? Why, man, of course, wonderful man ... You ever read poetry? No, of course you wouldn't.

Ironically, Hammer's subsequent investigation into her death and his route, so he thinks, to wealth, depend upon a clue based on a Christina Rossetti poem, the solution to which equates the female body with a threatening corruption of the flesh.

An aura of futility presides over his investigation, best expressed by Hammer's secretary Velda (Maxine Cooper): '"They"? A wonderful word. And who are they? They are the nameless ones who kill people for the great whatsit. Does it exist? Who cares? Everyone everywhere is so involved in the fruitless search for ... what?'. These lines, dubbed over the image in post-production, seem to have been delivered from too close to the microphone. Consequently, a speech that diegetically merely questions Hammer's continuing pursuit of the case also sounds like a voice-over. If these are actually Velda's unspoken thoughts, then the already-fragmented diegesis has fragmented sufficiently to permit a female character interiority and subjectivity; if this speech is a voice-over directly addressed to the audience, then it constitutes an even more damning indictment of Hammer's violent course.

Film noir's recurring fragmentation and centrifugal disintegration of the subject is complemented by a strong sense of the subject constructed, moment by moment, on the site of the material body through the centripetal operation of various linguistic, discursive and ideological pressures, through multiple simultaneous, if contradictory, interpellations, including other characters' plots and manipulations.

This is exemplified in a pair of Lang's films. In *The Big Heat*, homicide sergeant Dave Bannion (Glenn Ford) is caught up in the workings, and machinations, of the corrupt city machinery when his investigation into a cop's suicide threatens to reveal collusion between organised crime, city government and the police. Warned off by his own superiors, he contemplates resigning. As his wife, Katie (Jocelyn Brando), tells him, 'Your big trouble, honey, is that you attack yourself from all sides, like Jersey mosquitoes.' His reply evokes a similar sense of being attacked from all sides, of being caught in a web regardless of what he does: 'What am I supposed to do, hold on to my job by just stringing along, afraid to look to the left or to the right, because I might see something that they don't want me to see.' This is reiterated by Katie's response – 'If you do, you're going to have trouble from me. Just keep leading with your chin and don't you compromise' – which indicates another conflicting set of expectations simultaneously working to interpellate him as a subject. He is, moment by moment, the product of an attempted reconciliation of multiple simultaneous determinants; and that Katie tells him precisely what he 'wanted to hear [her] say' does not prevent this positioning from being contradictory.

The conversations between Dave and Katie in the three sequences in their idealised home interweave his public-professional and private-personal interpellations, the latter developed through their carefully choreographed interactions and movement around each other. In the first sequence, Katie, with Dave's assistance, serves dinner, sipping from his whisky, dragging on his cigar, threatening to sip from his beer. This sense of the couple's subjectivity arising from their mutual intersubjectivity is equally evident, although more subtly developed, in the third sequence as they discuss Dave's dilemma while clearing up after a meal. This intersubjective construction of the subject within discourse is further developed when Dave half-sceptically quotes the child-rearing book as an authority on how they should behave towards their daughter, Joyce (Linda Bennet), while Katie points out that the authors have not met Joyce. Within the constraints of gendered labour and divisions of public and private realms, Dave and Katie together attempt to negotiate their way through various interpellative systems while, at the same time, mutually interpellating each other. When Katie is killed, blown up by a car-bomb intended for Dave, he hands in his badge, separating himself from one of the contradictory interpellative systems which has governed so much of his life and in which he no longer has any faith. The remainder of the film is as much concerned with his reintegration into, and repositioning within, dominant discourses as it is about his pursuit of Katie's killers. The various characters who come to his aid temporarily perform the kinds of negotiating and repositioning previously undertaken by Katie. Debby Marsh (Gloria Grahame), the girlfriend of gangster Vince Stone (Lee Marvin), is aware of some of the determining interpellations to which she is subjected. She jokingly compares Vince and his cronies to circus animals, jumping when syndicate boss Mike Lagana (Alexander Scourby) cracks the whip. She is extremely conscious of her good looks, recognising that they alone give her access to material well-being. When Vince throws boiling coffee in her face (significantly, this happens just after she has taken a sip from his glass), scarring her for life, she knows she will be repositioned accordingly. Before taking her revenge, she kills Bertha Duncan (Jeanette Nolan), freeing Dave to be reintegrated. The film concludes with Debby's death and Dave's return to work. Without Katie as a counterbalance, and with Debby unavailable as an alternative, this dénouement is only possible because the evidence released by Bertha's death has swept all corruption from the city. This improbable conclusion is undermined by the final line of the film, in which Dave tells one of the cops to keep the coffee hot. This callous forgetting of Debby suggests other lacunae beneath Dave's superficially secure repositioning within now-benevolent interpellations.

A similar sense of multiple-interpellating determinants can be found in *While the City Sleeps*, a film which can be understood as a kind of riposte to *Citizen Kane* (1941). As Michael Walker argues, Lang is more 'interested in the network of relationships' surrounding the patriarch, Amos Kyne (Robert Warwick), and 'in the question of what happens when the patriarch dies' – a 'concern … with continuity' both within and 'between the personal and the social' (1992c: 69) which enables the film to explore the complex determinations and interactions of subjects and events. In a precisely-edited nineteen-shot sequence, described in detail below, television news-analyst Edward Mobley (Dana Andrews) addresses serial killer Robert Manners (John Barrymore, Jr), a subject caught in a complexly interwoven discursive web:

Shot 1 [In the office of Mark Loving (George Sanders), Mobley's fiancée Nancy Liggett (Sally Forrest) turns on the television. An announcer intones the programme's introduction.] Mr Walter Kyne presents the distinguished author, columnist and Pulitzer Prize-winner Edward Mobley in his perceptive analysis of the day's news. [The camera pans slightly to include Loving, who has just returned from putting the story on the newswire, in the shot as Mobley begins.] Ladies and gentlemen, at approximately 3am this morning in our city...

Shot 2 [Mobley, sat behind his desk in the television studio, shot from behind the crew.] ...one human being took the life of another. In our world, acts of violence are not rare, and so my excuse...

Shot 3 [Medium shot of Mobley, roughly corresponding with the television camera's viewpoint.] ...I should say my reason – for giving importance to this particular story is my hope that...

Shot 4 [Medium-long shot of Manners, in his pyjamas and sat backwards on a chair, facing his television, which is positioned in the bottom-left corner of the frame.] ...the killer may be listening to me, for I believe, that in his progress to the chair or to the insane asylum, that he's reached a way-station where his sick and warped ego...

Shot 5 [Shot from over Manners' left shoulder. Mobley's direct address to the television camera appears as a direct address to Manners.] ...demands to be fed with the milk of self-importance. And so with the consent of a very good friend of mine...

Shot 6 [The office of Lieutenant Kaufman (Howard Duff). In a shot whose composition resembles that of shot 4, he is sitting with his feet on his desk, sideways onto his television which is positioned in the bottom-left corner of the frame.] ...who's by way of being a remarkable criminologist but who has also asked that his name not be credited...

Shot 7 [The television studio, as shot 2.] ...I am going to say a few things to the killer, face...

Shot 8 [Manners' bedroom in long-shot. The camera is more-or-less side-on to the killer, positioned behind and to his left so as place him and the television at opposite sides of the screen, with his head and the television on the same level.] ...to face. Item 1: Mr Unknown, you will not for very long remain...

Shot 9 [Medium shot square on to Manners.] ...unknown. Item 2:...

Shot 10 [Shot of Manners' television, almost filling the frame.] ...you're husky, strong enough to have choked to death this morning...

Shot 11 [As shot 9.] ...the poor school teacher by the name of Laura Kelly. Item 3:...

Shot 12 [As shot 10, but the television camera tracks in on Mobley, ending in a close-up.] ...you are the same killer who last week bludgeoned to death a girl by the name of Judith Felton.

Shot 13 [As shot 9; as the shot ends, Manners drops his comic book.] You are the Lipstick Killer. Item 4: you read the so-called comic books.

Shot 14 [Close-up of the dropped comic book on the floor between Manners' feet. It is *The Strangler*, the same comic as was found at the scene of Kelly's murder.] Item 5: You have dark brown hair.

Shot 15 [As shot 5.] A few strands of your hair were found beneath the fingernails of your latest victim.

Shot 16 [As shot 9.] Item 6: you are young. A crime lab examination of your hair reveals that you are approximately twenty years of age. Item 7:...

Shot 17 [As shot 12, but the television camera has finished tracking in and Mobley is in close-up.] ...you're a mamma's boy.

Shot 18 [Close-up of Manners.] Item 8: the normal feeling of love that you should have toward your mother has been twisted into hatred for her and all...

Shot 19 [As shot 8. There is a knocking on the door.] ...of her sex. Item 9:... [Manners leaps up to switch off the television, hide *The Strangler* and pick up a textbook.]

This sequence, through its editing and shot composition, produces a clear sense of the various relationships which structure Mobley's life, and of the various interpellative apparatuses brought to bear on Manners, constructing him in certain ways. It produces an elaborate structure around a central absence – the confrontation between Mobley and Manners that is not a confrontation, an intersubjective moment that is not an intersubjective moment, which lacks reciprocity and takes place nowhere. Mobley is situated by his past (an ex-crime journalist, he is still friends with Kaufman); his relationships with his virtuous fiancée, who is also Loving's secretary, and the more experienced women's columnist Mildred Donner (Ida Lupino), who is romantically involved with Loving; his professional and personal relationships with the three senior figures at the Kyne news organisation – Loving, head of the wire service, John Day Griffith (Thomas Mitchell), editor of Kyne's flagship newspaper, and Harry Critzer (James Craig), head of Kyne Pix – who, at the instigation of Walter Kyne, Jr (Vincent Price), after inheriting his father's business, are competing for the new post of executive director by trying to crack the Lipstick Killer case. This competition is complicated by Kyne's dislike for Mobley, whom Amos Kyne had regarded as a son and more appropriate successor, and by Critzer's affair with Kyne's wife, Dorothy (Rhonda Fleming). This complex web interpellates Mobley and variously determines him. More pointedly, the sequence described above locates and constructs him at the intersection of various gazes and positionings: an elite media personality, a person to be filmed, a colleague, a lover, a romantic rival, a professional rival, a friend and, for Manners, a complex of powerful father and marginalising institutions who accuses, taunts, reprimands and knows too much. Meanwhile, the increasingly agitated Manners is subjected to/by a direct but unreciprocal address which constructs him as subordinate to and determined by powerful institutions (the media, the police) and discourses around deviance (juvenile delinquency, homosexuality).

Mobley's description of Manners is, to a certain extent, confirmed in the following sequence. Manners was adopted (his adoptive father then abandoned the family) and suffers from a gender-confusion: 'When you adopted me, you wanted a girl, didn't you? And he wanted a boy. Well, neither one of you were satisfied, were you? I remember once when I was eight years old, eight years old, I was helping you dust the house, and that woman from across the street came over and said, "My, my", and you said, "Yes, I know – he's exactly like a little girl, isn't he?"'. His mother's reply – 'But Robert, you are my son and my daughter and all the children I ever wished I could have had' – seems to confirm the source of his confusion and sense of inadequacy.

However, the proposition that an absent father, smothering mother and gender-confusion turned Manners into a killer is at least partially disrupted by an elaborate series of parallels with both Mobley and Walter. Walker's discussion of the connections between Mobley and Manners links the former's 'sexual desire' with the latter's 'murderous desire' (1992c: 62), with Manners the Id to Mobley's Ego. As Amos Kyne's portrait suggests, he was, like Manners' father, a continually present absence who structured his son's life through, among other things, contrasting him with the idealised Mobley (his other child, his business empire, for which he becomes an absent presence, is similarly discontented). The relationships between Mobley and Amos, Mobley and Griffith, and Critzer and Walter follow similar Oedipal trajectories. What this patterning suggests is that similar determinants produce similar but different subjects – that subjects are the over-determined products of multiple, often contradictory, interacting determinants – and that the mechanisms of social repression are generally sufficient to moderate the subject. For example, while none of the male characters treat women well, only one of them becomes a killer. The others settle for more everyday misogynies.

Complex determinism is central to the heist movie. An inversion of the investigation film, it focuses on the attempt to construct and control future events rather than retrospectively reconstruct and master past events. Both *The Asphalt Jungle* and *The Killing* foreground a sensitive dependence on initial conditions. In the former, after the heist he planned has gone badly wrong, wounded Doc Riedenscheider (Sam Jaffe) bemoans the arbitrary and unpredictable: 'You put in hours and hours of planning, figure everything down to the last detail, then what? Burglar alarms start going off all over the place for no sensible reason. A gun fires of its own accord and a man is shot. And a broken-down old harness bull, no good for anything but chasing kids, has to trip over us. Blind accident, what can you do against blind accident?' In the latter, the importance of initial conditions is made clear when Johnny Clay (Sterling Hayden) says, 'This is a rough drawing of the track as I remember it. Randy, you'll have to get me an A1 street map of the whole district. George, Mike, I want you to go over this thing with me inch by inch. Bring it completely up to date, add or subtract the slightest change, even if it's something as small as the placing of a hot-dog stand.' However, the film's complex temporal ordering and authoritative voice-over as it follows the various gang members mocks the orderliness Clay tries to impose on a world of which he cannot have perfect or, ultimately, even sufficient knowl-

edge. He can anticipate neither the chain of events, resulting from a necessary improvisation, which end in the death of Nikki Arane (Timothy Carey),
nor the counterplot which ends in the rest of the gang being shot. He is
then undone by airline regulations, a suitcase with a faulty lock and a yappy
little dog. As the police close in, his girlfriend Fay (Coleen Gray) urges him
to run, but he is as resigned to, or as complicit in, his fate as *The Killers'*
Swede a decade earlier. Mistaking the complex determinants which have
brought him to this moment for an inescapable fate, Clay relinquishes his
attempted mastery, shrugs and says, 'Ah, what's the difference?'

The above discussion of the film noir subject draws on the model of ideology proposed by Louis Althusser, in which he argues that the individual
subject is positioned or interpellated by the way ideology hails him or her.
Althusser's most famous attempt to illustrate this hailing was to imagine a
policeman calling out in the street, 'Hey, you there!', and 'the hailed individual will turn round. By this mere one-hundred-and-eighty-degree physical conversion, he becomes a subject. Why? Because he has recognised
that the hail was "really" addressed to him, and that "it was really him who
was hailed" (and not someone else)' (Althusser 1971: 163). This model has
often been criticised as being 'too rigid and mechanistic', incapable of producing 'a subject who is anything more than passive and manipulated by
discourse' (Bould 2002: 76). However, Althusser does allow for greater flex-
ibility than is normally credited:

> Each hailing positions the individual as a subject, but each hailing
> is in tension with every other hailing's attempt to position the indi-
> vidual as a subject. The subject, then, is not to be considered as a
> singular point, a monadic intersection, through which all hailings
> pass, but as a cluster or cloud of positions, constantly shifting and
> repositioning in response to each new hailing. (Bould 2002: 76–7)

This complex and never-resolved process is illustrated by the broadcast
sequence from *While the City Sleeps* discussed above, in which characters
are positioned by multiple discourses, institutions and relationships. A
further source of ambiguity, which leaves the determinism of Althusser's
model intact but renders it less mechanistic than many of its critics have
supposed, is exemplified by *Gilda*, a film that relies upon double-meanings,
coded significations and motivations which are neither quite conscious nor

unconscious. This repeated foregrounding of the fact that words have more than one meaning demonstrates that all hailings by discourse or ideology are rather more contingent than Althusser's policeman's yell.

In exotic Buenos Aires, bedraggled gambler Johnny Farrell (Glenn Ford), who knows 'about American sailors', is rescued from a mugging by dapper, effete Ballin Munson (George Macready) who is, for no clear reason, prowling 'a neighbourhood like this' at night. There follows a flirtatious exchange. Ballin describes his sword-cane as 'a most faithful and obedient friend ... silent when I wish it to be silent, it talks when I wish it to talk', to which Johnny replies that he 'must lead a gay life'. Later, at Ballin's illegal casino, Johnny offers to become another such friend. Before agreeing, Ballin seeks reassurance 'that there is no woman anywhere', and they then drink a toast to the three of them – Johnny, Ballin and the sword-cane. The queer coding of their affectionate relationship runs throughout the film, even after Ballin returns from a trip with Gilda, his new wife and, unknown to Ballin, Johnny's former lover. This introduces an Oedipal triangle, evident in Johnny's voice-over when he stalks out of Ballin's house: 'It was all I could do to walk away. I wanted to go back up in that room and hit her. What scared me was I ... I wanted to hit him, too. I wanted to go back and see them together with me not watching. I wanted to know.' He is constructed as a subject by and in his conflicting desires – for departure and return, for Gilda and for Ballin, for sex and for violence, for vision and invisibility, for presence and absence. In a subsequent toast to the three of them, Gilda has replaced the sword-cane, simultaneously usurping the homosexual desire it signified and replacing it with a sexualised mother figure to whom Johnny is denied access.

Double-coding and linguistic contradictions multiply. When Gilda and Johnny talk about dancing, they seem to mean sex. When Gilda, Ballin and Johnny talk about hate, they seem to mean sexual desire or, possibly, love. To provoke Johnny, Gilda puns that if she had 'been a ranch, they'd have called [her] the Bar Nothing'. Elsewhere she suggests psychoanalytic interpretations of words, as when Johnny compares her to Ballin's dirty laundry, and of actions – 'I can never get a zipper to close; maybe that stands for something'. Gilda gives two very different renditions of 'Put the Blame on Mame', a song which blames various disasters on women. The first performance, private and low-key, works to undermine this equation; the second, public and spectacular, seems to confirm it; but in combination, and because of all that we have seen happen between these renditions, they reveal it – and the femme fatale – as misogynist fantasies enabling masculine disavowal of desire and responsibility.

This polysemic play indicates language's ambiguity and therefore the potential ambiguity of discursive interpellations. Depending on multiple contexts, they can be misunderstood, misinterpreted and deflected, and so, even as they work to position the subject, contradictions emerge. The moment-by-moment emergent subject is simultaneously forming and, as in Captain Delgado's (Gerald Mohr) description of Johnny, 'breaking up in little pieces right in front of my eyes'.

As this chapter's examples have demonstrated, film noir repeatedly shows us that the subject is an emergent phenomenon within a total system, and that the subject's continuity is produced by an ongoing retrospective telling of the self; but, as with the total system, minor fluctuations can cause rapid and substantial divergences. The next chapter will give a brief account of the development of neo-noir which is a partial, retrospective and abstracted narrative, neither true nor false. It will conclude with a discussion of *Femme Fatale*, a neo-noir which consciously works with an idea drawn from non-linear dynamics (chaos theory): the sensitive dependence on initial conditions.

4   AGAINST ALL ODDS: NEO-NOIR

Batty scanned across the search wreckage that lapped up against the
replicas of Frank Lloyd Wright's original *faux* Mayan wall panels.

– K. W. Jeter (1995: 235)

If a single definition capable of producing a clear sense of where film
noir's boundaries lie remains elusive, then defining neo-noir is even
more difficult. Because Siodmak's *The Killers* includes not only Damico's
triangular relationship, but also a woman-as-mystery, a femme fatale, a
seeker-hero, a victim-hero, a homoerotic investigation, gangsters, boxing,
revenge against the mob, a couple on the run, a heist, and so on, then
other films containing some of these elements have been described as film
noirs. They also contain other elements shared by still other films, causing
the genre to flourish from multiple centres. With the passage of time, the
genre took on fresh concerns and, through the same process, exfoliated
further, becoming fuzzier, harder to pin down. This prompts a range of
questions: Are film noir and neo-noir the same or different genres? Are all
new crime films, because they cannot help but refer to film noir in some
way, to be considered neo-noirs? Can one identify a dominant tendency
within a film which renders it ineluctably noir? Or can one talk about any
film as noir if it is illuminating to do so, regardless of what one might
consider its dominant generic tendency? For example, imagine a trapped
man pursued through an office building by those who wish him harm while
he attempts to thwart their schemes. If this is *The Big Clock* (1948), then it

is a film noir; if it is *No Way Out* (1987), the remake, then calling it a neo-noir is relatively unproblematic; but when it is *Die Hard* (1988), generic identification becomes more vexed. *Die Hard*'s film noir elements include a semi-official investigator who represents an older order of masculinity – a blue-collar, vest-toting, western-quoting cop (and father) – endangered by a new order of femininity and feminised masculinity represented by his imperilled executive wife, her yuppie colleagues and the designer villains; a racial anxiety shapes its depictions of the Japanese and various feminised black men, and when John McLane (Bruce Willis) finally meets Sergeant Al Powell (Reginald VelJohnson) the homoerotic undercurrents bubble up to the surface. And yet something about this Christmas action-movie blockbuster seems to militate against labelling it noir – perhaps not so much the spectacular scale of the film or its happy ending (after all, the main cycle included some A-movies and happy endings) as the reactionary white male American supremacism it articulates. As with Siegel's *The Killers*, then, there are reasons to put it near the centre of noir, and reasons to marginalise or exclude it.

With these problems in mind, this final chapter will sketch in film noir's impact on British and French cinema, before turning to a brief treatment of some of the trends and developments in nearly four decades of neo-noir, a treatment characterised by numerous necessary omissions. The chapter will close with an extended discussion of *Femme Fatale*, a film symptomatic of the current condition of Anglophone neo-noir.

Film noir in Britain and France

In Britain, the crime film developed a noirish sensibility, most evident in such adaptations of Greene's fiction as *Brighton Rock* (1947), *The Fallen Idol* (1948) and *The Third Man* (1949), the latter two directed by Carol Reed, who also directed the noirish *Odd Man Out* (1947) and *The Man Between* (1953). Something of this sensibility can also be detected in Ealing Studio's *Kind Hearts and Coronets* (1949), *The Lavender Hill Mob* (1951) and *The Ladykillers* (1955), although it is worked out in a thoroughly British manner derived from a tradition of grotesque and gothic comedy about social class. This dialectical interplay of British and American models is evident in the contrast between the heist movie *The Good Die Young* (1954) and the caper movie *The League of Gentlemen* (1960). The latter, with its all-British cast, is a closely-observed comedy about a class system it simultaneously despises and valorises. It is torn between pulp plebianisation and nostalgia for hierarchical deference. The former film, in which several of the major roles are played by Americans (Richard Basehart, Gloria Grahame, John Ireland) is a glummer affair which activates class in a much more superficial way. Washed-up boxer Mike (Stanley Baker), who understands and accepts his class position, is residual, a glitch in the fantasy of atomised classlessness and social mobility.

Baker is the nearest Britain came to producing a noir leading man, giving powerful and subtle performances in *Hell Drivers* (1957), *Hell is a City* (1960), *Blind Date* (1959) and *The Criminal* (1960). (The latter pair were directed by Joseph Losey, one of a number of HUAC exiles who contributed something noirish to British crime films, including Edward Dmytryk and Jules Dassin, who directed *Obsession* (1949) and *Night and the City* (1950), respectively.) Baker's film noirs constitute an intriguing series of interactions between Anglo-American crime traditions and British realist film aesthetics, interactions which culminate in *Get Carter* (1970), the most significant neo-noir reworking of the unofficial investigator motif and revenge-against-the-mob plot. (Other – American – reworkings include *Point Blank* (1967; remade as *Payback* (1999)), *The Outfit* (1974) and *The Limey* (1999).)

As the main noir cycle ran its course, its impact was clearly felt in French crime movies and thrillers, like Jacques Becker's *Touchez pas au Grisbi* (1945) and *Casque d'Or* (1952); Henri-Georges Clouzot's *Quai des Orfèvres* (1947), *Le Salaire de le peur* (1953) and *Les Diaboliques* (1954); René Clément's *Au-delà des grilles* (1949) and *Plein Soleil* (1959); exiled Jules Dassin's *Du Rififi chez les hommes* (1955); Louis Malle's *Ascenseur pour l'echefaud* (1957); Robert Bresson's *Pickpocket* (1959); and Jean-Pierre Melville's *Bob le Flambeur* (1955), *Deux hommes dans Manhattan* (1959), *Le Doulos* (1962) and *Le Samouraï* (1967). Film noir and American crime cinema in general were important influences on a number of New Wave directors. Claude Chabrol directed *Le Beau Serge* (1958), *Le Boucher* (1969) and *Que la bête meure* (1969). François Truffaut adapted a David Goodis novel as *Tirez sur le pianiste* (1960) and two Woolrich novels as *La Mariée était en noir* (1967) and *La Sirène du Mississippi* (1969); his final film, *Vivement dimanche* (1983) was adapted from a Charles Williams novel. Jean-Luc Godard transformed the heist movie into *Bande à part* (1964) and worked variations on the couple-on-the-run scenario in *A Bout de souffle* (1960),

Pierrot le fou (1965) and *Weekend* (1967). His most noirish film, *Alphaville* (1965), blends a Lemmy Caution *policier* with the European dystopian tradition to produce the first major science fiction neo-noir.

Neo-noir: a sketch

Despite such late examples of the heist movie as *Charley Varrick* (1973) and *The Friends of Eddie Coyle* (1973), it was clear, as early as *Ocean's Eleven* (1960) and *Topkapi* (1964), that the imperatives of post-classical film-by-film production were transforming it into the spectacular, star-centred, action-driven, sometimes comic, caper movie, from *The Anderson Tapes* (1971) and *The Taking of Pelham One Two Three* (1974) to *Mission: Impossible* (1996) and the re-make of *Ocean's Eleven* (2001). Following the American *Reservoir Dogs* (1992) and the British *Lock, Stock and Two Smoking Barrels* (1998), the heist movie underwent a resurgence – *Heat* (1995), *Dead Presidents* (1995), *Face* (1997), *Croupier* (1999), *Sexy Beast* (2000) – but one can discern in each of these examples tensions between low-key and high concept, between film noir and blockbuster aesthetics. Arguably, these tensions shaped neo-noir's development. There is a clear sense in the late-1960s and early-1970s that, as film noir emerged as a recognised and recognisable genre, it represented a pre-sold concept to be repackaged and resold.

Several films returned to hard-boiled sources, such as the Chandler adaptations *Marlowe* (1969), *The Long Goodbye* (1973), *Farewell, My Lovely* (1975) and *The Big Sleep* (1978). The first and third are particularly instructive. *Marlowe* gave James Garner an opportunity to rehearse the updated private eye he would perform so effectively in *The Rockford Files* (1974–80), and although such films have since been plentiful, the character type now belongs to television. *Farewell, My Lovely* represents two affiliated trends: the period or costume noir, ranging from *Chinatown* (1974) to *LA Confidential* (1997); and the noir remake, including films as various as *Thieves Like Us* (1974), *The Postman Always Rings Twice* (1981), *Against All Odds* (1984), *D.O.A.* (1988), *Desperate Hours* (1990), *Cape Fear* (1991), *Night and the City* (1992) and *The Deep End* (2001), several of which are also period pieces. (Costume noir need not be period noir; see, for example, *Blade Runner* (1982) or *The Usual Suspects* (1995).) While neo-noir can often be seen in terms of the loss of historicity in postmodern culture anatomised by Fredric

Jameson (1991), this is not to say that their nostalgia precludes critique. For example, the refraction of the Watergate scandal through *Chinatown*'s fictionalised retelling of William Mulholland's 1906 'Rape of Owens Valley' frequently seems like a retreat from political engagement. However, Evelyn Mulwray's (Faye Dunaway) denial that her father raped her, which implies that their daughter is the product of consensual incest, might be a startling momentary indictment of the complicity of those protesting Richard Nixon's misrule.

The clearest examples of this ahistorical tendency are the films of Joel and Ethan Coen. While others continued to adapt hard-boiled crime writers – such as Jim Thompson in *The Kill-Off* (1990), *The Grifters* (1990), *After Dark, My Sweet* (1990), *The Getaway* (1994), *This World, Then the Fireworks* (1997) – the Coens made hard-boiled 'adaptations' not actually based on particular novels. *Miller's Crossing* (1990) is their Hammett story, *The Big Lebowski* (1998) their Chandler; *Blood Simple* (1984) and *The Man Who Wasn't There* (2001) are their Cains, perhaps retold by Thompson. Like the many film noirs that yearned for an earlier stage of capitalism and older versions of masculinity, the Coens register a profound dissatisfaction with the present but, as *The Hudsucker Proxy* (1994) shows, they know that the clock cannot really be turned back. Like their eponymous *Barton Fink* (1991), a writer who is unable to write, they are unable to slingshot this impasse, and so their films, which often seem hermetic and disconnected, become exquisitely-crafted comedies of this self-knowledge. For example, in *Miller's Crossing*, Tom Reagan (Gabriel Byrne), the enigmatic lieutenant of mobster Leo (Albert Finney), plays out his role in the gang-war as if it were nothing more than a role, a predetermined function. Everything he does – from falling for Verna (Marcia Gay Harden), Leo's squeeze, to stoically accepting a beating from his bookie's henchmen – is done with no sense of interiority. Although he occasionally loses control of events, his self-possession, his mastery of his self, is expressed through confident, sometimes ornate, hard-boiled dialogue; when he is most in danger – when Eddie Dane (J. E. Freeman) takes him to Miller's Crossing, intending to execute him, and when Eddie turns up at the wrong moment in Johnny Caspar's (Jon Polito) office – he clams up, lost for words. But the Coens' clever pastiche of hard-boiled prose – like the barren, almost cartoonishly sketched-in *mise-en-scène* and the panoply of parodic characters – evokes an entextualised past rather than historicity, a performance rather than an identity; and their embrace of past and performance is ultimately consolatory, mostly.

Several varieties of noir story seem to have been especially popular among neo-noir filmmakers. The gangster film thrived in the long shadows cast by Francis Ford Coppola and Martin Scorsese. New manifestations of the femme fatale can be found in a whole range of neo-noirs, from *Body Double* (1984) to *Bound* (1996), but the character type featured most prominently in direct-to-video and made-for-cable films, many of them erotic thrillers, with John Dahl's *Red Rock West* (1992) and *The Last Seduction* (1994) premiering on cable before receiving theatrical releases. Among the many couples-on-the-run and other neo-noir road movies are *Badlands* (1973), *Wild at Heart* (1990), *Thelma & Louise* (1991), *True Romance* (1993), *Natural Born Killers* (1994), *Freeway* (1996), *Breakdown* (1997), *Buffalo 66* (1998) and *Joy Ride* (2001). This turn to non-urban spaces has produced a number of rural and smalltown neo-noirs, including *One False Move* (1992), *Fargo* (1996), *A Simple Plan* (1998) and *U Turn* (1997). In *Mean Streets* (1973) and *Taxi Driver* (1976), Martin Scorsese depicted a fractured and disorientated masculinity, while Abel Ferrara's *The Driller Killer* (1979), *Ms.45* (1981), *Fear City* (1984), *King of New York* (1990), *Bad Lieutenant* (1992), *Dangerous Game* (1993), *The Addiction* (1995) and *The Blackout* (1997), exposed the breakdown of the American city, the collapse of consensual moral order, the paranoia and brutality of late-capitalism and the fucked-up gendered subjects, especially men, it produces. His *New Rose Hotel* (1998) is a science fiction neo-noir, a subgenre partially enabled by the way 1980s cyberpunk science fiction embraced film noir and hard-boiled crime fiction (and unpacked the noirishness at the core of Philip K. Dick's science fiction). Other examples include *Naked Lunch* (1991), *Equinox* (1993), *Dark City* (1998) and *The Thirteenth Floor* (1999).

The *Strassenfilm* reappeared as the yuppie nightmare movie (*After Hours* (1985), *Desperately Seeking Susan* (1985), *Something Wild* (1986), *Judgment Night* (1993), *Se7en* (1995), *Very Bad Things* (1998)), becoming po-faced in Michael Douglas vehicles like *Fatal Attraction* (1987) and *Falling Down* (1993). For good or ill, Douglas, who also starred in *Coma* (1978), *The Star Chamber* (1983), *Black Rain* (1989), *The War of the Roses* (1989), *Basic Instinct* (1992), *Disclosure* (1994), *The Game* (1997) and *A Perfect Murder* (1998) is the major neo-noir leading man. (Tom Berenger runs him a close second. Although a number of actresses, like Kathleen Turner,

Sharon Stone and Linda Fiorentino, have made several neo-noirs, none of them have become so closely identified with the genre, perhaps because of Hollywood's preference for youthful leading ladies and neo-noir's for female nudity.)

Basic Instinct, along with films like *Body of Evidence* (1993) and *Jade* (1995), signal an attempt to relocate the erotic thriller from video or cable to cinema screens. However, it is a genre at which Anglophone cinema is singularly inept. Occasionally an Anglophone erotic thriller might muster some eroticism or thrills, and might even manage, albeit often unwittingly, to be remotely interesting about sexual attraction, sexuality and gender, but most are weakened by the tendency to mistake the spectacular eroticised display of female nudity for a challenging engagement with ideas about and representations of sexuality. They are further undone by the desire to avoid the NC-17 rating, which is almost certain to prohibit exhibition in lucrative mall theatres (see Sandler 2002, Williams 2004). In contrast to such easy-viewing, the treatments of sexual obsession found, for example, in Tsukamoto Shinya's films about sex, mortality, violence and transformation – the most obviously noirish being *Tokyo-ken* (1995), *Bullet Ballet* (1998), *Rokugatsu no hebi* (2002) and *Vital* (2004) – are far more compelling. Uncomprehending of complacency and bloat, they trouble.

Although dream sequences and subjective world-distortions played an important role in film noir and its expressionist antecedents – recall, for example, the hyperbolic dream worlds of *Der Letzte Mann* (1924) or *Stranger on the Third Floor* – it is only really with neo-noirs like *De Vierde man* (1983), *Angel Heart* (1987), *Jacob's Ladder* (1990), *Suture* (1993), *Lost Highway* (1997), *The Gift* (2000), *Ôdishon* (2000), *Mulholland Drive* (2001) and *Fear X* (2002) that fantasy becomes a central noir element, materialising many of those things that film noir had only been able to suggest. And so this sketch will close with a discussion of two films from different decades which offer some insight into this turn to the fantastic and which have accrued a similar cult status: David Lynch's *Blue Velvet* (1986) and David Fincher's *Fight Club* (1999).

In *Blue Velvet*, Jeffrey Beaumont (Kyle MacLachlan) is drawn into an underworld of violence, horror, crime and police corruption he never suspected existed in his small home-town. He finds a severed ear and his subsequent unofficial investigations lead him to singer Dorothy Valens (Isabella Rossellini), whose husband and child have been abducted by the crazed Frank Booth (Dennis Hopper) so as to force her to comply with his desire to repeatedly rape her. The film recapitulates various film noir elements, including a woman in peril and the opposition between a sexualised mother and an innocent daughter, in a highly self-conscious manner. Stilted dialogue, mannered performances, pastiches of 1950s melodramas and teen movies, visual distortions, extreme close-ups, slow-motion and theatrical square-on compositions all alienate the viewer from the diegetic illusion, making the film's edgier material seem more confrontational than it would otherwise necessarily be. At the core of the film is a Freudian primal scene fantasy, depicting more or less explicitly what *Gilda*'s Johnny so desperately desired (to hit Gilda, to hit Ballin, to see them together with him not watching). Jeffrey spies on Dorothy as she strips to her underwear; she attacks him with a knife; she fellates him; Frank arrives and Jeffrey must hide, almost naked, in the closet and watch while Frank, who seems to switch between father and child roles, beats and rapes Dorothy. The fluidity of subject positions forced upon or played by each of the characters in this sequence articulates something of the trauma central to psychoanalytic accounts of subject formation.

A similar argument can be made about the misogyny of *Fight Club*. In order for Narrator (Edward Norton) to become a 'real' man, he must be separated from the supposedly effeminate realm of consumerism and side with Tyler Durden (Brad Pitt), his father-figure ego-ideal who also happens to be a figment of his imagination, against Marla Singer (Helena Bonham-Carter), a sexualised mother-figure with whom 'Tyler' has frequent, noisy and energetic sex. It is only through over-identifying with his 'father' that Narrator is able to construct a sufficiently strong identity to then reject Tyler's proto-fascist homoerotic masculinity and perhaps form a more normative heterosexual couple with Marla. Throughout the film, Tyler speaks with absolute confidence, regardless of the adolescent platitudes, frequently mistaken for a radical critique of capitalism, he spouts, while Narrator struggles with language: at the various therapy groups he attends, he depends upon his own silence so as to give nothing of himself away; around Marla, he becomes tongue-tied; and he begins to talk about himself in the third person. From a Lacanian perspective, he only enters the symbolic realm when he begins to speak as Tyler would; but this increasing over-identification with his father must be brought to a traumatic conclusion. In trying to prevent Project Mayhem's destruction of the headquarters of several credit card companies, Narrator begins to identify with patriarchy rather than his father. Marla's personality has altered according to the requirement of any particular scene, and it shifts once more as the skyscrapers fall and as Narrator reaches for her hand: now that her man knows his place, she knows hers.

Neo-noir now: a snapshot, a rebus

Because *Femme Fatale* is little-known, it is necessary to begin with a lengthy plot-description (which will help to capture something of the flavour of this convoluted and absurd film). It starts with a caper at the 2001 Cannes Film Festival. Veronica (Rie Rasmussen) is wearing a $10 million 'off-the-shoulder top', little more than a diamond encrusted band of yellow gold coiled around her breasts and upper torso like a serpent. She is picked up by a woman, who might be called Laure Ash (Rebecca Romijn-Stamos). Intercut with the caper's other carefully-choreographed shenanigans, they begin to have sex in a toilet cubicle; as Laure drops each item of Veronica's clothing/jewellery to the floor, Black Tie (Eriq Ebouaney) switches them for duplicates. When he is briefly distracted, the double-cross kicks in, with Laure returning the duplicate top to him. Wounded, Black Tie is left behind as Laure escapes. She meets her girlfriend in Belleville. They are photographed by Nick Bardo (Antonio Banderas) and spied on by Black Tie's henchman, Racine (Edouard Montoute). Sheltering in a church, Laure is 'recognised' by the funeral congregation. Followed by the concerned Irma (Eva Darlan) and Louis (Jean-Marie Frin), she makes for room 214 at the Charles De Gaulle Sheraton to collect a new passport. Racine attacks her, throws her from a balcony. Irma and Louis take her, unconscious, to a cosy apartment. Once awake and alone, she explores her surroundings.

By an astonishing coincidence, Laure is identical to Lily (also played by Romijn-Stamos), whose husband and daughter recently died. Laure finds Lily's passport and an aeroplane ticket, but as she starts to drowse in the bath, the bereft Lily returns and kills herself. Laure takes her identity and, *en route* to the US, meets Bruce Hewitt Watts (Peter Coyote), a millionaire who works for the State Department. Seven years later, he becomes the American Ambassador to France, and he takes Laure, now his wife Lily, with him.

Bardo, a reluctant paparazzo, is hired to photograph 'Lily Watts'. Black Tie, released from gaol, and Racine set about tracking down Laure. They find her girlfriend in Belleville, and throw her in front of a passing truck, killing her. They pick up Laure's trail from Bardo's photograph, now the cover of *Gala* magazine. Bardo spots Laure, dark glasses hiding a black eye, and follows her, tailed by Black Tie and Racine. Bardo sees Laure buy a gun and follows her to the Sheraton, room 214. Convinced she is suicidal, he cons his way into the room. After he talks her out of suicide, she seduces him, steals his keys and sends him to replace her asthma medication. To ensure that she cannot leave or kill herself, he takes her clothes and the gun with him in her car. Laure anonymously phones the police, who arrest Bardo. They do not believe his story, but Watts makes them drop all charges. Laure emails a ransom note from Bardo's account, making it look like he has kidnapped her. Wanting no part of her plan to con Watts out of $10 million, Bardo tries to warn him, but Laure shoots them both. Black Tie and Racine appear, and throw her into the Seine. She falls, suddenly naked, into eerily clear water, and swims for the surface, only to wake up in the bath in Lily's apartment. It has all been a dream.

This time, Laure intervenes in Lily's suicide, persuading her that she will meet a man on the aeroplane and fall in love. A truck driver (Salvatorre Ingoglia) gives Lily a lift to the airport. She gives him a pendant that belonged to her daughter; he hangs it in his cab to remind him of his own daughter. Seven years later, in Belleville, Laure collects the money from

FIGURE 7 Old and new: *Femme Fatale*

FIGURE 8 Off-the-shoulder top: *Femme Fatale*

selling the diamonds from her girlfriend. They agree to go their separate ways. Bardo watches and photographs as Laure's girlfriend is captured by Black Tie and Racine. This time, when they throw her in front of the truck, the sun appears from behind the clouds, reflects off the pendant hanging from the driver's mirror, dazzling him. He swerves, missing her and killing Black Tie and Racine. Laure's girlfriend is revealed to be Veronica. Bardo helps Laure to her feet. When he asks if they have met before, she replies, 'Only in my dreams'.

 Femme Fatale opens with the final confrontation between Neff and Phyllis from *Double Indemnity*, playing on television with French subtitles. Reflected in the screen is Laure, lying on her bed, apparently naked, propped up on one elbow as the camera slowly tracks out and past her. Coming late in the history of film noir, it is appropriate that the film should open like this as this is how film noir was fabricated: in French and by the recirculation of old films in new venues. Laure's reflection superimposed over *Double Indemnity* – a palimpsest, a hieroglyph – connotes the proximity of, and distance between, Phyllis and Laure. Film noir's sexual undercurrents are made visible even as the psychosexual intensity made possible by their proscribed visibility fades, like a black-and-white ghost, beneath a mandated and spectacular visibility. In *Femme Fatale*'s first sex scene, haunted by the shower sequence from *Psycho* (1960), Veronica's near-naked body is pressed against the semi-opaque, screen-like cubicle wall – but if this is an attempt to cover the visible so that the invisible can be recovered, it fails. The clock cannot be turned back.

In the third volume of Swift's *Gulliver's Travels* (1726), Gulliver encounters the fabulous Lagadan machine. Intended to aid authorship in many different disciplines 'without the least assistance from genius or study', it produces random groups of words; when there are 'found three or four words together that might make part of a sentence' they are recorded in volumes out of which the Professor intends to construct a 'complete body of all arts and sciences' (1963: 221–2). This device depends upon recombining syntagmatic elements so as to produce new syntagms which can then be organised into a new whole. This is not unlike Brian De Palma's method, as his *constructions en abîme* – his texts within the text – suggest.

One variety of filmic *construction en abîme* is the incorporation into the diegesis of 'painterly or graphic forms of representation' which, because they are 'sharply differentiated from the texture of the film thanks to the way they are encoded ... seem to flaunt the fact that they are representations' (Iampolski 1998: 37). The most obvious example of this in *Femme Fatale* is the wall-sized collage of the Belleville junction Bardo has constructed

FIGURE 9 Collage: *Femme Fatale*

from hundreds of overlapping photographs shot over at least seven years. Like the film, it is constructed out of quotations, captured moments; and, in fabricating a totality by spatialising the passage of time, it calls attention to the textuality of film itself. The substratum of film is the photogram (see Stewart 1999), the individual image or frame which is made invisible when projected as part of a film. The still photograph – *Femme Fatale* is full of still photographs – is a trace of and allusion to the photogram; and the photogram itself is arguably a model of film quotation and intertextuality, of the disruption of a text's linearity. Mikhail Iampolski quotes Laurent Jenny:

> What is proper to intertextuality is the introduction of a new mode of reading that explodes the linearity of the text. Each intertextual reference is the site of an alternative: either one keeps reading, seeing the reference as nothing more than one fragment among others, an integral part of the text's syntagmatics; or one returns to the original text, resorting to a kind of intellectual anamnesis whereby the intertextual reference appears as a 'displaced' paradigmatic element issuing from a syntagmatic axis that has been forgotten. (1998: 30)

There is, then, a tension between whether the film can offer sufficient narrative motivation for the presence of a particular syntagm (or syntagmatic element), or whether one is driven to 'seek its motivation in some other logic or explanatory cause outside the text ... in the realm of intertextuality' (ibid.). These fragment-alternatives in *Femme Fatale* include the following. The foregrounding of a key, a bag, Laure's changing hair colour and Bardo's camera recall Hitchcock, especially *Notorious*, *Psycho*, *Marnie* (1964) and *Rear Window*, while the prominence given to photography recalls Antonioni's *Blow-Up* (1966), which De Palma reworked as *Blow Out* (1981). Laure's mysterious identity, her shadowing by Bardo and the Bernard Herrmann-like score recall *Vertigo*, which De Palma reworked as *Obsession* (1976). The intersection in the French countryside where Racine collects Black Tie recalls *North by Northwest* (1959). The recollection of *Psycho*'s shower sequence alluded to above recalls De Palma's several reworkings of it in *Carrie* (1976), *Dressed to Kill* (1980) and *Blow Out*. The it-was-all-a-dream explanation recalls Lang's *The Woman in the Window*, as well as De Palma's *Body Double*. Laure's sudden appearance behind a hotel maid and the deaths of Black Tie and Racine recall moments from De Palma's *Raising Cain* (1992). Racine's descent down a duct during the caper recalls a sequence in De Palma's *Mission: Impossible*, itself reworking a sequence from Dassin's *Topkapi*. Lily and Laure embody film noir's good-woman/bad woman dichotomy – like the twin sisters of Siodmak's *The Dark Mirror*. Like Jeff in Tourneur's *Out of the Past* and like Swede and Johnny in their respective versions of *The Killers*, Laure's past catches up with her by chance. The shadows of the blinds in the police interrogation room recall countless film noir settings. Bardo is every schmuck who ever fell for a crooked dame. And so *Femme Fatale* is bathed in recognition, always-already known; but can it simultaneously amount to more than the mere sum of its (borrowed) parts?

Iampolski argues that where an anomalous fragment which the film cannot convincingly integrate 'violates the calm of mimesis' we can 'begin to see vigorous traces of semiosis' (ibid.). The intertextual fragment which is foregrounded (or perhaps merely recognised) is like the photographic still in the film which evokes the photogram: just as the film is composed of photograms (and Bardo's collage of photographs), so the text is composed of intertextual fragments. While the photogram exposes the film's textuality, the fragment exposes its intertextuality. When a fragment disrupts the linear narrative flow, 'we witness the birth of meaning, which is normally transparent wherever mimesis remains untroubled, dissolving into the effortless movement from signifier to signified'; by violating this mimetic link the quoted fragment orients 'the sign toward another text rather than a thing' (ibid.). One variant of this process, in which the viewer has more agency than Iampolski seems to suggest, can be found in Bardo's performance of a gay man, a non-threatening guise he adopts to gain access to Laure's hotel room. It is so embarrassingly bad that it draws attention to itself; and one desperately seeks an intertextual motivation which might somehow excuse, or at least, mitigate it (perhaps it is a nod to the effeminate persona Bogart's Marlowe adopts in *The Big Sleep*'s bookshop sequence, already reworked in *Blade Runner*).

Femme Fatale's other *construction en abîme* is the dream which occupies the majority of the film. As if to provide us with a viewing protocol for the film, De Palma packs the dream with clues about its status. Laure falls asleep in an overflowing bath with the taps still running at 3.33pm, according to the clock in the bathroom. Throughout the dream, we are returned to this moment by an overflowing fishtank, recurring images of water being poured, a painting of a waterfall, various bath-like blue rectangles of blue, a poster for *Deja Vue* (note the unusual feminine ending) which features John Everett Millais's painting of a drowning *Ophelia* (1851–52), over whose face Laure's is superimposed; and by clocks which all tell the same time – 3.33pm. Several objects from the frame story – such as the flashing pharmacy sign, Veronica's camouflage outfit – recur, and various actors reappear, sometimes playing different roles. But what is significant is that the dream also seems to leak out into the frame tale.

One function of the it-was-all-a-dream explanation (which has been present as a possibility throughout for the observant viewer) is to excuse the ridiculous plot and the many ludicrous moments it contains (Black Tie is released from gaol in the blood-stained tuxedo he was wearing when captured; Laure fakes a black eye so as to get Bardo to follow her; and so on). However, the dream is no more ridiculous than the frame tale (Black Tie hinges the caper on Laure's ability to pick up Veronica with a single whispered comment; Laure and Lily look identical; and so on). The traffic between dream and frame, hypodiegesis and diegesis, returns us to Bardo's collage, which does exist, unseen by Laure, in the frame tale before and after her dream. Its presence seems to confirm that Laure's dream was a vision of her future if she did not save Lily; but then what is the function of the smaller photo-collage on Lily's pinboard, if not a prompt for Laure to dream Bardo's collage?

Femme Fatale demonstrates a sensitive dependence upon initial conditions: within complex systems microscopic fluctuations can produce macroscopic divergences (see also *Lola rennt* (1998) and *Memento* (2001), as well as William Tenn's 'Brooklyn Project' (1948) and Ray Bradbury's 'A Sound of Thunder' (1952), science fiction short stories concomitant with the main cycle of film noir). Laure's decision to intervene in Lily's suicide shuts down the alternative plot which resulted in both their deaths. Unknown to Laure, the fluctuation she introduced by saving Lily would result in Lily giving the pendant to the truck driver thus, seven years later, saving Veronica, killing Black Tie and Racine and introducing Laure to Bardo.

Although *Femme Fatale* produces a conservative vision of non-linear dynamics (the only significant differences between the dream version and frame version of the closing incident at Belleville are the presence of Laure and the pendant – as if Laure's seven years in France and Lily's in the US have produced no fluctuations, have had no consequences), this is necessary, if one wishes to foreground issues of determinism: a wildly divergent system militates against any sense of dénouement. In following the model offered by Tenn, Bradbury and numerous other counterfactual fictions, in which a minor alteration produces an alternative history which diverges from the history we know but not so radically as to be unrecognisable, *Femme Fatale* is caught between the same irreconcilable impulses towards systemic openness and narrative closure; and it therefore models the text in the image of Tiresias, the mythical 'blind androgyne ... chosen by the gods to bear forever a memory that would not fade' who, in Eliot's 'The Waste Land', 'throbb[ed] between two lives' (Iampolski 1998: 2, 3).

There is a hint of this in Bardo's name, which recalls 'bardo', the name Tibetan Buddhism gives to the intermediate stage between death and rebirth. On one level, this might be a complex allusion to *Vertigo*. (Although based on Pierre Boileau and Thomas Narcejac's novel *D'entre les morts* (1954), *Vertigo* was also partly inspired by Ambrose Bierce's 'An Occurrence at Owl Creek Bridge' (1886). In this short story, a hanged man miraculously escapes his execution and returns home; but the conclusion reveals that his escape and return were a fantasy in the final moments of his life. At the start of *Vertigo*, Scottie is left dangling in the air with no obvious means of escape; at the end of the film, he stares into the abyss. This has prompted some critics to suggest that, following Bierce, the intervening narrative is merely a dream. Regardless of whether this is case, throughout the film Scottie is caught between states in a metaphorical bardo.) On another level, it is a lesson about neo-noir.

Like Scottie, like Lily when she holds the gun to her head and like Laure when she watches, like Bardo as he waits for the perfect moment to photograph, like text itself, neo-noir is suspended between states. If film noir is a partial and abstracted narrative trajectory (neither necessary nor sufficient, but nonetheless useful sometimes) that is retrospectively fabricated in order to make sense of a wider system's moment-to-moment transition, so neo-noir's intertextual fragments constitute the ongoing fabrication of that trajectory. To mix metaphors, the neo-noir film is the collapsing wavefront, stitching itself into a narrative trajectory and webbing itself into an intertext. Open and closed, looking forward and back, inward and outward, it is perpetually in bardo.

AFTERWORD: KISS TOMORROW GOODBYE

> It was two thirty in the morning, and raining. In the City, it was always
> two thirty in the morning and raining ... But I was still strapped into
> my life, bound by a plot I could no longer predict, condemned to
> ride the streetcar until the last stop.
>   – Kim Newman (1989: 3 & 37)

Like all good monsters, film noir escaped.

Often reduced to little more than an image or an idea – the city at night,
the femme fatale – it is a touchstone of popular culture. From the 1985
Moonlighting episode, 'The Dream Sequence Always Rings Twice' and the
1986 *Dick Spanner, P.I.* animations to the 2003 computer game *Max Payne
2: The Fall of Max Payne*, allusions to this familiar megatext are readily
perceived and understood. It is little wonder, then, that when the alien
Strangers of *Dark City* construct an environment in which to perform their
experiments upon abducted humans they choose to build and rebuild the
eponymous locale.

Mike Wayne argues that German expressionism and American film noir
lack lucidity because of an 'existential crisis' derived from the subject's
'incomprehension' in the face of the 'absurd and impenetrable world'
(2003: 216) of commodity fetishism and reification. In contrast, he suggests
that *Dark City* is 'hyperconscious of the politics of its intertextual cultural
references'; but he nonetheless notes in it 'that sense – difficult to pin
down empirically – that the aesthetics have become, like the subjects in the
film, a shell or bodily form emptied of the emotional power and substantive

historical content/context that originally motivated them' (2003: 216–7). As the world Wayne describes has become no less absurd or impenetrable since the middle of the twentieth century, it is not unreasonable to conclude that contemporary noir aesthetics and allusions now perform, among other things, a consolation. They offer an image of the world that, however distorted, is familiar and comprehensible. This consolatory tendency can be best explained in terms of the double logic of remediation, by which 'our culture wants to both multiply its media and to erase all traces of mediation' (Bolter and Grusin 1999: 5), and by briefly considering two neo-noirs from either end of the budgetary spectrum of contemporary digital filmmaking: *This Is Not a Love Song* and *Sin City*.

Although screened at festivals as early as January 2002, *This Is Not a Love Song* officially premiered on 5 September 2003, when it was simultaneously released in UK cinemas and on-line (the website received over a hundred thousand hits during its opening weekend). Shot for less than £300,000 in just twelve days, using a handheld Sony PD150 camera and DV tape, it refashions the couple-on-the-run plot in *Deliverance* (1972) territory. Taciturn ex-soldier Heaton (Kenny Glenaan) collects his excitable young friend Spike (Michael Colgan), just released from a four-month prison sentence for stealing £57, and takes him on a road trip in a stolen car. When they run out of petrol in the middle of nowhere, a farmer, mistaking Heaton for a thief, locks him up at gunpoint. Spike gets hold of the shotgun, but accidentally shoots and kills the farmer's daughter, Gerry (Keri Arnold). Outraged locals divert the police search to London and then hunt Heaton and Spike across desolate moorland. As Heaton fails to get Spike to safety and, injured, has to rely on him more and more, so their relationship becomes increasingly fraught. With their pursuers closing in, Heaton begs Spike to carry him. They tussle. Spike hits Heaton on the head with a rock, leaving him for dead. Spike is taken by the locals, gagged, bound and drowned. The locals trace Heaton to a narrow cave and seal him up inside. Somehow, he survives and escapes but, like *Vertigo*'s Scottie, he is left confronting an emotional and psychological abyss.

Sin City was shot on high-definition video in front of a green screen, with many of the actors not actually meeting each other despite sharing scenes. Costing $40 million, it took $120 million worldwide in the first four months of its cinematic release. The portmanteau film is based on four of Frank Miller's 1990s 'Sin City' comics – 'The Customer is Always Right', 'That

Yellow Bastard', 'The Hard Goodbye' and 'The Big Fat Kill' – which delight in belonging to the crude pulp tradition of Mickey Spillane and garish paperback covers: Sin City is the kind of place where all the women are whores and all the whores are beautiful, capable of handling a gun and taking a punch.

In the opening vignette, The Man (Josh Hartnett) tells a beautiful woman that he loves her, then assassinates her. In the next story, Hartigan (Bruce Willis), an about-to-retire honest cop crippled by angina, rescues 11-year-old Nancy (Makenzie Vega) from paedophilic serial killer Roark Jr (Nick Stahl), the son of Senator Roark (Powers Boothe). In the next story, set eight years later, the seemingly indestructible Marv (Mickey Rourke) is framed for the murder of a prostitute, Goldie (Jaime King). Because she was nice to him, he sets out to find her killer, eventually teaming up with Goldie's identical twin sister and fellow prostitute, Wendy (Jaime King). The trail leads him via other murdered prostitutes and Kevin (Elijah Wood), their cannibal killer, to Cardinal Roark (Rutger Hauer). Marv mutilates and murders the Cardinal, and is executed. In the next story, Dwight (Clive Owen) finds himself caught up in a mob scheme to regain control of Old Town, which is run by the prostitutes who work there. When Gail (Rosario Dawson), their leader and Dwight's ex-lover, is abducted, he must set a trap in which they can brutally slay the mobsters. The film then returns to Hartigan. Senator Roark paid to keep him alive so as to force him to confess to Roark Jr's crimes. Hartigan refused, but was convicted anyway as no-one would allow Nancy to testify. She promised to write to him in prison. Eight years later, Hartigan receives a severed finger rather than his weekly letter. Convinced Nancy (Jessica Alba) is in danger again, he confesses and is immediately released. He tracks her down– she is a stripper and, she declares, in love with him – but it has all been a set-up to lead Yellow Bastard (Nick Stahl) to her. Hartigan again rescues her – Yellow Bastard is Roark Jr, horribly transformed by the chemical processes involved in replacing the genitals Hartigan shot off eight years earlier. Hartigan beats him to death and tears off his new genitals. Fearing that Nancy will be caught up in Senator Roark's revenge, Hartigan shoots himself in the head. In the closing vignette, The Man offers Becky (Alexis Bledel), the prostitute who betrayed Old Town to the mob, a cigarette.

Despite their very obvious differences, these two films indicate the problem Wayne notes of the relationship between an aesthetics and its socially, culturally and historically specific contexts while pursuing the double and contradictory logics of remediation. Jay Bolter and Richard Grusin argue that 'although each medium promises to reform its predecessors by offering a more immediate or authentic experience, the promise of reform inevitably leads us to become aware of the new medium as a medium' (1999: 19). This contradiction is evident in *This Is Not a Love Song*'s intertwining of realist and expressionist techniques. At times shot with almost Dogme-like purity, the hand-held camera prowls around the action, often getting that little bit too close to the characters, sometimes losing focus, other times refocusing abruptly. Elsewhere, the film expressionistically distorts the image: blurs of colour replace the landscape through which the stolen car races; slow-motion disrupts the relationship between the image and diegetic sound; sat in front of a café window, Heaton and Spike are reduced to little more than silhouettes; when the panicked Spike brandishes the shotgun, he is filmed with a camera mounted on it; when Spike inhales an aerosol, he trips in day-glo colour. However, even as both sets of techniques claim a form of unmediated immediacy, they also draw attention to the medium mediating. While the handheld 'realist' camera places the viewer in the midst of the action, its shakiness, shifts of focus, zooms out and natural lighting are not merely aesthetic choices evocative of certain varieties of realism but also reminders that the camera being used is not so different from home video technology. Furthermore, in its positioning – whether in close proximity to the characters or, for example, half underwater as they hide in a river gorge – it becomes an expressive realism, emphasising a noirish entrapment. Meanwhile, the more obviously mediated and expressionist images – the blurred landscapes, the day-glo tripping – also suggest a direct and unmediated corporeal experience of speed or drugs.

This contradiction is mirrored in the relationship between Heaton and Spike. The insistence of PIL's plaintive 'This Is Not a Love Song', which recurs throughout, unleashes the homoeroticism of both this particular story and film noir more generally. But the film simultaneously draws attention to the mechanisms of denial and suppression that fuel both it and the genre. Gerry is the only woman in the film. Fifteen years old, she is an unlikely potential third point to a noir love triangle; but even with the early removal of any threat she might pose to the men's relationship, their feelings for each other can never be articulated. They talk incessantly, but say very little. Early on, Heaton denies having missed Spike while he was

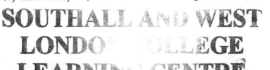

in prison, but then their exchange of glances as they argue over the radio becomes flirtatious, and their subsequent wrestling verges on becoming something else. When they spot the city that might offer them sanctuary, Heaton gazes lovingly at Spike as he gleefully dances. At night, they sleep curled around one another, untroubled by this physical intimacy. Both live in fear of being abandoned by the other. Most poignant of all is Heaton's voice-over as, at various moments, we hear the opening lines of the many letters he tried to write to the imprisoned Spike but could never complete. The ambiguities of this relationship are never pinned down or named. The film instead gives us a sense of these characters' immediacy to each other, while the mechanisms of shot construction and voice-over mediate that experience for the viewer, making their relationship at once both simple and complex.

Sin City is more noteworthy for its attempt to recreate the distinctive visual style than the narratives of its sources. Miller has spoken of the influence of comic artists Johnny Craig and Wallace Wood and, especially, Will Eisner's 'The Spirit' comic strip (1940–52), although stylistically he seems most indebted to Kazuo Koike and Goseki Kojima's violent 1970s manga *Kozure Okami* (*Lone Wolf and Cub*). The 'Sin City' comics are drawn in stark black-and-white, often with the simplicity of woodcuts. Long sequences are presented with little written text – for example, the 26-page 'Silent Night' contains one sound effect and a single speech bubble – while other pages are overburdened with words, with panels cramped by packed speech bubbles and long columns of text running down a thick margin. As Miller remediates the hardboiled novel in comic book form, the visual image claims a greater immediacy even as the intermittent excesses of text point to the inadequacies of the visual image at capturing aspects of the hardboiled novel. Similarly, the *Sin City* film uses digital tools to give its viewer the immediacy of the comic book image. However, there is again a contradiction. As the digital film remediates the comic book, the immediacy on offer is the product of hypermediation. By 'recreating' Miller's simple illustrations – some of which are displayed in the title sequence – the medium draws attention to, rather than effaces, itself.

In addition to the image, the film remediates Miller's written text as voice-overs which become so excessive that, at one point, Dwight seamlessly takes over his internal monologue, speaking it aloud within the diegesis. Unlike *This Is Not a Love Song*, in which the voice-over fractures

FIGURE 10 Noir image: *Sin City* (2005)

Heaton's superficially confident and competent masculinity, this sequence displays *Sin City*'s hysterical investment in psychic unity and continuity. Whereas the former film plays with and explores the homoeroticism of film noir, the latter reduces sexuality to displays of elaborately costumed gun-toting prostitutes, an armed and naked lesbian parole officer and a stripper packing six-shooters, betraying a not entirely unconscious homosexual panic through the over-performance of heterosexual masculinity and repeated assaults, both verbal and physical, on male genitals.

However, it is not merely the comic book that *Sin City* remediates. In many spectacle-driven movies, computer-generated imagery (CGI) is utilised to show everything, to render entire worlds visible, as with the vertiginous depths of the city in *Star Wars: Episode 2 – Attack of the Clones* (2002). But this impulse is frequently denied in *Sin City* as it uses digital technology to recreate analogue effects. For example, in the opening vignette, which is set on a roof terrace high over the city, the background is often out of focus behind the sharp foreground images of the actors. Similarly, when Hartigan drives to the waterfront to rescue young Nancy, he does so in front of a digitally created backdrop which looks like an old-fashioned back-projection. Both of these immediacy-effects are instructive in that they do not claim to offer a more direct experience of the real but, like the verité camerawork in *This Is Not a Love Song*, a familiar and thus authenticating visual language or representation. At other times, *Sin City*'s seems anxious about such recreations, becoming overly parodic, even cartoonish. At these moments, the impulse to erase the new medium 'so that the viewer stands in the same relationship to the content as she would if she were confronting the original medium' (Bolter and Grusin 1999: 45) conflicts with the impulse 'to emphasise the difference rather than erase it' (1999: 46), as the opening vignette makes clear. As The Man holds the woman he has killed, the image switches to a white-on-black silhouette, replicating a frame from 'The Customer Is Always Right'. This comic book moment is followed by a crane shot that only CGI could achieve, the virtual camera rising up from the roof terrace, spiralling around skyscrapers and up into the sky to look down on this Manhattan-like district whose contours spell out 'Sin City' in a font familiar from Miller's comic books.

Returning to Wayne's argument about the hollowed-out aesthetics of *Dark City*, one can see in *Sin City*'s simple linear narratives and one-dimensional characters a reduction of film noir to its image(s) and the desire not to make a film noir but to somehow put the very idea, the megatext, of film noir on the screen. In contrast, *This Is Not a Love Song* creates an aesthetics out of economic necessity, cannibalising past styles while innovating at the edges of what its technology permits (for example, the tripping sequence consists of colour-reversed footage shot with an off-the-shelf digital lens which could operate detached from the body of the camera and thus could be fixed to the end of a fishing rod). In this sense, *This Is Not a Love Song* is a film noir while *Sin City* merely looks like one.

This judgement, however, too closely matches a knee-jerk preference for 'realist' over 'fantastic', 'independent' over 'studio', low-budget over big-budget, European over Hollywood filmmaking to be persuasive. These rough binaries should rather be seen as different modes through which film noir continues to evoke the absurd and impenetrable world of late capitalism. For all its ambiguities, *This Is Not a Love Song* is a love story, although its protagonists are trapped within the socially-constructed subjectivities which deny their love. Likewise, the crude certainties of *Sin City* – its depictions of armoured masculinity and eroticised femininity, its various detectives' ability to trace crimes to unambiguous individual sources – are so hyperbolic, the milieu so knowable, as to completely separate this hermetic metrocosm and its continuous, unified subjects from reality. And even though the realist impulse and aesthetics of *This Is Not a Love Song* might seem to directly address 'existential crisis', it is through its various remediations that it becomes as effective an expression as *Sin City* of a cultural moment which shies away from exploring depth. Both films fetishise surface and superfice, generating what complexity they can from the proliferation of images and sounds. If their aesthetics are empty shells, they nonetheless connect to the moment.

Such remediations are recommodifications, images and styles repackaged and resold as capital exfoliates across levels and dimensions. But the remediation of film noir in digital films is something else, too. It is the next stage in the fabrication of the genre. To see *This Is Not a Love Song* and *Sin City* as film noirs requires us to look backward so as to validate their inclusion in the genre. Just as the Strangers reconstruct their *Dark City* every night to introduce small variants which might produce massive changes, so each additional film noir rethinks, reconstructs and refabricates the genre. For all the superficial unity implied by the certainty of *Sin City*'s visual style and by yet another book about the genre, film noir, like the subjects it depicts, is discontinuous and disunified – strapped into and bound by a plot no one could predict, condemned to ride the streetcar until the last stop.

FILMOGRAPHY

À bout de souffle (*Breathless*) (Jean-Luc Godard, Fr., 1959)

Ace in the Hole (Billy Wilder, US, 1951)

The Addiction (Abel Ferrara, US, 1995)

After Dark, My Sweet (James Foley, US, 1990)

After Hours (Martin Scorsese, US, 1985)

Against All Odds (Taylor Hackford, US, 1984)

Algiers (John Cromwell, US, 1938)

Alphaville (Jean-Luc Godard, Fr./It., 1965)

The Anderson Tapes (Sidney Lumet, US, 1971)

Angel Heart (Alan Parker, US/Can./UK, 1987)

Angels with Dirty Faces (Michael Curtiz, US, 1938)

Ascenseur pour l'echefaud (*Lift to the Scaffold*) (Louis Malle, Fr., 1957)

Asphalt (Joe May, Ger., 1928)

The Asphalt Jungle (John Huston, US, 1950)

L'Atalante (Jean Vigo, Fr., 1934)

Attack (Robert Aldrich, US, 1956)

Au-delà des grilles (*Beyond the Gates*) (René Clément, Fr. 1949)

Baby Face (Alfred E. Green, US, 1933)

Badlands (Terrence Malick, US, 1973)

Bad Lieutenant (Abel Ferrara, US, 1992)

Ball of Fire (Howard Hawks, US, 1941)

Bande à part (*Band of Outsiders*) (Jean-Luc Godard, Fr., 1964)

Barton Fink (Joel Coen, US/UK, 1991)

Basic Instinct (Paul Verhoeven, US/Fr., 1992)

Beast of the City (Charles Brabin, US, 1932)

Le Beau Serge (*Handsome Serge*) (Claude Chabrol, Fr., 1958)

La Belle équipe (*They Were Five*) (Julien Duvivier, Fr., 1936)

Bend of the River (Anthony Mann, 1952)

La Bête humaine (*The Human Beast*) (Jean Renoir, Fr., 1938)

Beware, My Lovely (Harry Horner, US, 1952)

Beyond a Reasonable Doubt (Fritz Lang, US, 1956)

Beyond the Forest (King Vidor, US, 1949)

The Big Clock (John Farrow, US, 1948)

The Big Heat (Fritz Lang, US, 1953)

The Big Lebowski (Joel Coen, US/UK, 1998)

The Big Sleep (Howard Hawks, UK, 1946)

The Big Sleep (Michael Winner, US, 1978)

The Black Cat (Edgar G. Ulmer, US, 1934)

The Blackout (Abel Ferrara, US/Fr., 1997)

Black Rain (Ridley Scott, US, 1989)

Blade Runner (Ridley Scott, US, 1982)

Der Blaue Engel (Josef von Sternberg, Ger., 1930)

Blind Date (Joseph Losey, UK, 1959)

Blood Simple (Joel Coen, US, 1984)

Blow Out (Brian De Palma, US, 1981)

Blowup (Michelangelo Antonioni, UK/It., 1966)

The Blue Dahlia (George Marshall, US, 1946)

The Blue Gardenia (Fritz Lang, US, 1953)

Blue Velvet (David Lynch, US, 1986)

Bob le Flambeur (Bob the Gambler) (Jean-Pierre Melville, Fr., 1955)

Body and Soul (Robert Rossen, US, 1947)

Body Double (Brian De Palma, US, 1984)

Body Heat (Lawrence Kasdan, US, 1981)

Body of Evidence (Uli Edel, Ger./US, 1993)

Boomerang! (Elia Kazan, US, 1947)

Le Boucher (*The Butcher*) (Claude Chabrol, Fr./It., 1969)

Bound (Larry and Andy Wachowski, US, 1996)

The Brasher Dubloon (John Brahm, US, 1947)

Breakdown (Jonathan Mostow, US, 1997)

Bride of Frankenstein (James Whale, US, 1935)

Brighton Rock (John Boulting, UK, 1947)

Buffalo 66 (Vincent Gallo, US, 1998)
Bullet Ballet (Shinya Tsukamoto, Jap., 1998)
Bullets or Ballots (William Keighley, US, 1936)
Cape Fear (J. Lee Thompson, US, 1962)
Cape Fear (Martin Scorsese, US, 1991)
Carrie (Brian De Palma, US, 1976)
Casablanca (Michael Curtiz, US, 1942)
Casbah (John Berry, US, 1948)
Casque d'Or (*Golden Marie*) (Jacques Becker, Fr., 1952)
Cat People (Jacques Tourneur, US, 1942)
Caught (Max Ophüls, US, 1949)
Cause for Alarm (Tay Garnett, US, 1951)
Champion (Mark Robson, US, 1949)
Charley Varrick (Don Siegel, US, 1973)
Chicago Deadline (Lewis Allen, US, 1949)
Le Chemin de Rio (Robert Siodmak, Fr., 1937)
La Chienne (Jean Renoir, Fr., 1931)
Chinatown (Roman Polanski, 1974)
Christmas Holiday (Robert Siodmak, US, 1944)
Citizen Kane (Orson Welles, 1941)
City Streets (Rouben Mamoulian, US, 1931)
Clash By Night (Fritz Lang, US, 1952)
Cloak and Dagger (Fritz Lang, US, 1946)
Coma (Michael Crichton, US, 1978)
Conflict (Curtis Bernhardt, US, 1945)
Convicted (Henry Levin, US, 1950)
Cornered (Edward Dmytryk, US, 1945)
Crack-Up (Irving Reis, US, 1946)
The Crazies (George A. Romero, US, 1973)
The Criminal (Joseph Losey, UK, 1960)
Criss Cross (Robert Siodmak, US, 1949)
The Crooked Way (Robert Florey, US, 1949)
Crossfire (Edward Dmytryk, US, 1947)
Croupier (Mike Hodges, Fr./UK/Ger./Ire., 1999)
Cry of the City (Robert Siodmak, US, 1948)
Cypher (Vincenzo Natali, US, 2003)
Dangerous Game (Abel Ferrara, US, 1993)

Dark City (Alex Proyas, US, 1998)
Dark Corner (Henry Hathaway, US, 1946)
The Dark Mirror (Robert Siodmak, US, 1946)
Dark Passage (Delmer Daves, US, 1947)
Dead End (William Wyler, US, 1937)
Dead Presidents (Allen and Albert Hughes, US, 1995)
Dead Reckoning (John Cromwell, US, 1947)
The Deep End (Scott McGehee, US, 2001)
Deliverance (John Boorman, US, 1972)
Le Dernier tournant (*The Last Turn*) (Pierre Chenal, Fr., 1939)
Desperate (Anthony Mann, US, 1947)
Desperate Hours (Michael Cimino, US, 1990)
Desperately Seeking Susan (Susan Seidelman, US, 1985)
Detour (Edgar G. Ulmer, US, 1945)
Deux hommes dans Manhattan (*Two Men in Manhattan*) (Jean-Pierre
  Melville, Fr., 1959)
Les Diaboliques (*Diabolique*) (Henri-Georges Clouzot, Fr., 1954)
Dick Spanner, P.I. (1986)
Die Hard (John McTiernan, US, 1988)
Dirnentragödie (*Tragedy of the Street* aka *Women Without Men*) (Bruno
  Rahn, Ger., 1927)
Disclosure (Barry Levinson, US, 1994)
D.O.A. (Rudolph Maté, US, 1950)
D.O.A. (Rocky Morton and Annabel Jankel, US, 1988)
Doktor Mabuse, der Spieler, Part, 1: Der grosse Spieler – ein Bild der Zeit
  (*Dr Mabuse, the Gambler*) (Fritz Lang, Ger., 1922)
*Doktor Mabuse, der Spieler, Part, 2: Inferno: Ein Spiel von Menschen
  unserer Zeit* (*Dr Mabuse, the Gambler*) (Fritz Lang, 1922)
The Doorway to Hell (Archie Mayo, US, 1930)
Double Indemnity (Billy Wilder, US, 1944)
Le Doulos (*Doulos: The Finger Man*) (Jean-Pierre Melville, Fr./It., 1962)
Dracula (Tod Browning, US, 1931)
Dressed to Kill (Brian De Palma, US, 1980)
The Driller Killer (Abel Ferrara, US, 1979)
Dr Jekyll and Mr Hyde (Rouben Mamoulian, US, 1932)
Du Rififi chez les hommes (*Rififi*) (Jules Dassin, Fr., 1955)
Easy Rider (Dennis Hopper, US, 1969)

Les Enfants du paradis (*Children of Paradise*) (Marcel Carné, Fr., 1943–45)
Equinox (Alan Rudolph, US, 1993)
The Ex-Mrs Bradford (Stephen Roberts, US, 1936)
Experiment Perilous (Jacques Tourneur, US, 1944)
Face (Antonia Bird, UK, 1997)
The Falcon Takes Over (Irving Reis, US, 1942)
The Fallen Idol (Carol Reed, US, 1948)
The Fallen Sparrow (Richard Wallace, US, 1943)
Falling Down (Joel Schumacher, Fr./US, 1993)
Farewell, My Lovely (Dick Richards, US, 1975)
The Far Country (Anthony Mann, US, 1955)
Fargo (Joel Coen, UK/US, 1996)
Fatal Attraction (Adrian Lyne, US, 1987)
Fear City (Abel Ferrara, US, 1984)
Fear X (Nicolas Winding Refn, Den./Can./UK/Braz., 2002)
Femme Fatale (Brian De Palma, Fr., 2002)
Fight Club (David Fincher, Ger./US, 1999)
The File on Thelma Jordan (Robert Siodmak, US, 1950)
The Finger Points (John Francis Dillon, US, 1931)
Footlight Parade (Lloyd Bacon, US, 1933)
Force of Evil (Abraham Polonsky, US, 1949)
Frankenstein (James Whale, US, 1931)
Freeway (Matthew Bright, US, 1996)
Die freudlose Gasse (*The Joyless Street*) (G. W. Pabst, Ger., 1923)
The Friends of Eddie Coyle (Peter Yates, US, 1973)
Fury (Fritz Lang, US, 1936)
The Game (David Fincher, US, 1997)
Gaslight (George Cukor, US, 1944)
Genuine (Robert Wiene, Ger., 1920)
The Getaway (Roger Donaldson, US/Jap., 1994)
Get Carter (Mike Hodges, UK, 1970)
The Gift (Sam Raimi, US, 2000)
Gilda (Charles Vidor, US, 1946)
The Glass Key (Frank Tuttle, US, 1935)
G-Men (William Keighley, US, 1935)
The Good Die Young (Lewis Gilbert, UK, 1954)
Le Grand Jeu (Jacques Feyder, Fr. 1933)

The Great Train Robbery (Edwin S. Porter, US, 1903)
The Grifters (Stephen Frears, US, 1990)
Gun Crazy (Joseph H. Lewis, US, 1949)
Hard To Handle (Mervyn LeRoy, US, 1933)
The Harder They Fall (Mark Robson, US, 1956)
Hangover Square (John Brahm, US, 1945)
Heat (Michael Mann, US, 1995)
Hell Drivers (Cy Endfield, UK, 1957)
Hell is a City (Val Guest, UK, 1960)
High Noon (Fred Zinnemann, US, 1952)
High Sierra (Raoul Walsh, US, 1941)
Hintertreppe – Ein Film-Kammerspiel (*Backstairs*) (Leopold Jessner, Ger.,
    1921)
His Kind of Woman (John Farrow, US, 1951)
Hôtel du Nord (Marcel Carné, Fr., 1938)
The House on 92nd Street (Henry Hathaway, US, 1945)
The Hudsucker Proxy (Joel Coen, UK/Ger./US, 1994)
Human Desire (Fritz Lang, US, 1954)
I Am a Fugitive from a Chain Gang (Mervyn LeRoy, US, 1932)
I Am the Law (Alexander Hall, US, 1938)
I Confess (Alfred Hitchcock, US, 1953)
I Drink Your Blood (David Durston, US, 1971)
In a Lonely Place (Nicholas Ray, US, 1950)
Ivy (Sam Wood, US, 1947)
I Wake Up Screaming (H. Bruce Humberstone, US, 1942)
Jacob's Ladder (Adrian Lyne, US, 1990)
Jade (William Friedkin, US, 1995)
Le Jour se lève (*Daybreak*) (Marcel Carné, Fr., 1939)
Joy Ride (John Dahl, US, 2001)
Judgment Night (Stephen Hopkins, US/Jap., 1993)
Das Kabinett des Dr. Caligari (*The Cabinet of Dr Caligari*) (Robert Wiene,
    Ger., 1919)
Keisatsukan (*Policeman*) (Uchida Tomu, Jap., 1933)
Key Largo (John Huston, US, 1948)
The Killers (Robert Siodmak, US, 1946)
The Killers (Don Siegel, US, 1964)
Killer's Kiss (Stanley Kubrick, US, 1955)

The Killing (Stanley Kubrick, US, 1956)
The Kill-Off (Maggie Greenwald, US, 1990)
Kind Hearts and Coronets (Robert Hamer, UK, 1949)
King Kong (Merian C. Cooper and Ernest B. Schoedsack, US, 1933)
King of New York (Abel Ferrara, It./US/UK, 1990)
King's Row (Sam Wood, US, 1941)
Kiss Me Deadly (Robert Aldrich, US, 1955)
Kiss of Death (Henry Hathaway, US, 1947)
Kiss Tomorrow Goodbye (Gordon Douglas, US, 1950)
Klute (Alan J. Pakula, US, 1971)
Kurutta Ippeiji (*A Page of Madness*) (Teinosuke Kinugasa, Jap., 1927)
L.A. Confidential (Curtis Hanson, US, 1997)
Ladies Love Brutes (Rowland V. Lee, US, 1930)
The Lady Eve (Preston Sturges, US, 1941)
The Lady from Shanghai (Orson Welles, US, 1948)
Lady in the Lake (Robert Montgomery, US, 1947)
The Ladykillers (Alexander Mackendrick, UK, 1955)
The Last House on the Left (Wes Craven, US, 1972)
Last Man Standing (Walter Hill, US, 1996)
The Last Seduction (John Dahl, US, 1994)
Laura (Otto Preminger, US, 1944)
The Lavender Hill Mob (Charles Crichton, UK, 1951)
The League of Gentlemen (Basil Dearden, UK, 1960)
Der Letzte Mann (*The Last Laugh*) (F. W. Murnau, Ger., 1924)
The Limey (Steven Soderbergh, US, 1999)
Little Caesar (Mervyn LeRoy, US, 1930)
Lock, Stock and Two Smoking Barrels (Guy Ritchie, UK, 1998)
The Lodger (John Brahm, US, 1944)
Lola rennt (*Run, Lola, Run* aka *Lola Runs*) (Tom Tykwer, Ger., 1998)
The Long Goodbye (Robert Altman, US, 1973)
The Long Night (Anatole Litvak, US, 1947)
Lost Highway (David Lynch, Fr./US, 1997)
The Lost Weekend (Billy Wilder, US, 1945)
Lured (Douglas Sirk, US, 1947)
M (Fritz Lang, Ger., 1931)
Macao (Josef von Sternberg [and Nicholas Ray, uncredited], US, 1952)
The Mad Miss Manton (Leigh Jason, US, 1936)

The Maltese Falcon (Roy Del Ruth, US, 1931)
The Maltese Falcon (John Huston, US, 1941)
The Man Between (Carol Reed, UK, 1953)
The Manchurian Candidate (John Frankenheimer, US, 1962)
Der Man, der Seinen Morder Sucht (*Looking for His Murderer*) (Robert
    Siodmak, Ger., 1931)
The Man from Laramie (Anthony Mann, US, 1955)
Man Hunt (Fritz Lang, US, 1941)
The Man Who Wasn't There (Joel Coen, US, 2001)
La Mariée était en noir (*The Bride Wore Black*) (François Truffaut, Fr./It.,
    1967)
Marlowe (Paul Bogart, US, 1969)
Marnie (Alfred Hitchcock, US, 1964)
The Mask of Dimitrios (Jean Negulesco, US, 1944)
La Maternelle (Marie Epstein, US, 1933)
Max Payne 2: The Fall of Max Payne (2003)
The Mayor of Hell (Archie Mayo, US, 1933)
Mean Streets (Martin Scorsese, US, 1973)
Medium Cool (Haskell Wexler, US, 1969)
Memento (Christopher Nolan, US, 2001)
Menschen am Sonntag (*People on Sunday*) (Robert Siodmak and Edgar G.
    Ulmer, Ger., 1930)
Metropolis (Fritz Lang, Ger., 1926)
Mildred Pierce (Michael Curtiz, US, 1945)
Miller's Crossing (Joel Coen, US, 1990)
Ministry of Fear (Fritz Lang, US, 1945)
Mission: Impossible (Brian De Palma, US, 1996)
Mollenard (*Hatred*) (Robert Siodmak, Fr., 1938)
Moonlighting (1985–89)
Ms.45 (Abel Ferrara, US, 1981)
Mulholland Drive (David Lynch, Fr./US, 2001)
Murder, My Sweet (Edward Dmytryk, US, 1944)
My Darling Clementine (John Ford, US, 1946)
My Name is Julia Ross (Joseph H. Lewis, US, 1945)
Nachts, wenn der Teufel kam (*Night, When the Devil Came* aka *The Devil
    Strikes at Night*) (Robert Siodmak, W.Ger., 1957)
The Naked City (Jules Dassin, US, 1948)

The Naked Kiss (Samuel Fuller, US, 1964)
Naked Lunch (David Cronenberg, Can./UK/Jap., 1991)
The Naked Spur (Anthony Mann, US, 1953)
Nancy Steele is Missing (George Marshall, US, 1936)
Natural Born Killers (Oliver Stone, US, 1994)
New Rose Hotel (Abel Ferrara, US, 1998)
Night and the City (Jules Dassin, UK, 1950)
Night and the City (Irwin Winkler, US, 1992)
Nightfall (Jacques Tourneur, US, 1957)
Nightmare Alley (Edmund Goulding, US, 1947)
A Night to Remember (Richard Wallace, US, 1943)
North by Northwest (Alfred Hitchcock, US, 1959)
Notorious (Alfred Hitchcock, US, 1946)
No Way Out (Roger Donaldson, US, 1987)
Obsession (Edward Dmytryk, UK, 1949)
Obsession (Brian De Palma, US, 1976)
Ocean's Eleven (Lewis Milestone, US, 1960)
Ocean's Eleven (Steven Soderbergh, US, 2001)
Odd Man Out (Carol Reed, UK, 1947)
Odds Against Tomorrow (Robert Wise, US, 1959)
Ôdishon (*Audition*) (Miike Takashi, Jap./S.Kor, 2000)
On Dangerous Ground (Nicholas Ray, US, 1952)
One False Move (Carl Franklin, US, 1992)
Orlacs Hände (*The Hands of Orlac*) (Robert Wiene, Ger., 1924)
The Outfit (John Flynn, US, 1974)
Out of the Past (Jacques Tourneur, US, 1947)
The Paradine Case (Alfred Hitchcock, US, 1948)
Payback (Brian Helgeland, US, 1999)
Pépé le moko (Julien Duvivier, Fr., 1936)
A Perfect Murder (Andrew Davis, US, 1998)
Per un pugno di dollari (*A Fistful of Dollars*) (Sergio Leone, W.Ger/Sp./It.,
    1964)
Phantom Lady (Robert Siodmak, US, 1944)
Pickpocket (Robert Bresson, Fr., 1959)
Pièges (*Personal Column*) (Robert Siodmak, Fr., 1939)
Pierrot le fou (Jean-Luc Godard, Fr./It., 1965)
Pitfall (Andre de Toth, US, v1948)

Plein Soleil (Purple Noon) (René Clément, Fr./It. 1959)

Point Blank (John Boorman, US, 1967)

The Postman Always Rings Twice (Tay Garnett, US, 1946)

The Postman Always Rings Twice (Bob Rafelson, US/W.Ger., 1981)

Psycho (Alfred Hitchcock, US, 1960)

The Public Enemy (William Wellman, US, 1931)

Pursued (Raoul Walsh, US, 1947)

Quai des brumes (Port of Shadows) (Marcel Carné, Fr., 1938)

Quai des Orfèvres (Quay of the Goldsmiths) (Henri-Georges Clouzot, Fr., 1947)

Que la bête meure (The Beast Must Die) (Claude Chabrol, Fr., 1969)

Racket Busters (Lloyd Bacon, US, 1938)

Raising Cain (Brian De Palma, US, 1992)

Ramrod (Andre de Toth, US, 1947)

Rancho Notorious (Fritz Lang, US, 1952)

Raskolnikov (Robert Wiene, Ger., 1923)

Raw Deal (Anthony Mann, US, 1948)

Rear Window (Alfred Hitchcock, US, 1954)

Rebecca (Alfred Hitchcock, 1940)

The Reckless Moment (Max Ophüls, 1949)

Red Rock West (John Dahl, US, 1992)

Remember Last Night? (James Whale, US, 1935)

Reservoir Dogs (Quentin Tarantino, US, 1992)

Ride the Pink Horse (Robert Montgomery, US, 1947)

Roadhouse Nights (Hobart Henley, US, 1930)

The Rockford Files (1974–80)

Rokugatsu no hebi (A Snake of June, Shinya Tsukamoto, Jap., 2002)

Rope (Alfred Hitchcock, US, 1948)

The Rough and the Smooth (Robert Siodmak, UK, 1959)

La Rue sans nom (Street Without a Name) (Pierre Chenal, Fr., 1933)

Le Salaire de le peur (The Wages of Fear) (Henri-Georges Clouzot, Fr./It., 1953)

Le Samouraï (Jean-Pierre Melville, Fr./It., 1967)

Satan Met A Lady (William Dieterle, US, 1936)

Scarface (Howard Hawks, US, 1932)

Scarlet Street (Fritz Lang, US, 1945)

Schatten – Eine nächtliche Halluzination (Arthur Robison, Ger., 1923)

Second Chance (Rudolph Maté, US, 1953)
Secret Beyond the Door (Fritz Lang, US, 1948)
Serenade (Anthony Mann, US, 1956)
The Set-Up (Robert Wise, US, 1949)
Se7en (David Fincher, US, 1995)
Sexy Beast (Jonathan Glazer, UK/Sp., 2000)
Shadow of a Doubt (Alfred Hitchcock, US, 1943)
Shane (George Stevens, US, 1953)
Sherlock Homes and the Voice of Terror (John Rawlins, US, 1942)
Shock Corridor (Samuel Fuller, US, 1963)
Side Street (Anthony Mann, US, 1950)
A Simple Plan (Sam Raimi, Fr./UK/Ger./US/Jap., 1998)
Sin City (Frank Miller and Robert Rodriguez, US, 2005)
La Sirène du Mississippi (*Mississippi Mermaid*) (François Truffaut, It./Fr.,
    1969)
Sleep, My Love (Douglas Sirk, US, 1948)
So Evil My Love (Lewis Allen, US/UK, 1948)
Something Wild (Jonathan Demme, US, 1986)
Somewhere in the Night (Joseph L. Mankiewicz, US, 1946)
Sorry, Wrong Number (Anatole Litvak, US, 1948)
Sous les toits de Paris (*Under the Roofs of Paris*) (René Clair, Fr., 1930)
The Spider Woman (Roy William Neill, US, 1944)
Spione (*Spies*) Fritz Lang, Ger., 1928)
The Spiral Staircase (Robert Siodmak, 1945)
The Star Chamber (Peter Hyams, US, 1983)
Star Wars: Episode 2 – Attack of the Clones (George Lucas, US, 2002)
Stella Dallas (King Vidor, US, 1937)
The Strange Affair of Uncle Harry (Robert Siodmak, US, 1945)
The Strange Love of Martha Ivers (Lewis Milestone, US, 1946)
Stranger on the Third Floor (Boris Ingster, US, 1940)
Die Strasse (*The Street*) (Karl Grune, Ger., 1923)
Street of Chance (John Cromwell, US, 1930)
Sudden Fear (David Miller, US, 1952)
Sunset Blvd. (Billy Wilder, US, 1950)
The Suspect (Robert Siodmak, US, 1945)
Suspicion (Alfred Hitchcock, US, 1941)
Suture (Scott McGehee, US, 1993)

Sweet Smell of Success (Alexander Mackendrick, US, 1957)

The Taking of Pelham One Two Three (Joseph Sargent, US, 1974)

Taxi Driver (Martin Scorsese, US, 1976)

Temptation (Irving Pichel, US, 1946)

Das Testament des Dr Mabuse (*The Testament of Dr Mabuse*) (Fritz Lang, Ger., 1933)

The Texas Chain Saw Massacre (Tobe Hooper, US, 1974)

Thelma & Louise (Ridley Scott, US, 1991)

They Live by Night (Nicholas Ray, US, 1948)

Thieves Like Us (Robert Altman, US, 1974)

The Thin Man (W.S. Van Dyke, US, 1934)

The Third Man (Carol Reed, UK, 1949)

The Thirteenth Floor (Josef Rusniak, Ger./US, 1999)

This Is Not a Love Song (Bille Eltringham, UK, 2002)

This World, Then the Fireworks (Michael Oblowitz, US, 1997)

Time to Kill (Herbert I. Leeds, US, 1942)

Tirez sur le pianiste (*Shoot the Piano Player*) (François Truffaut, Fr., 1960)

Tokyo-ken (*Tokyo Fist*) (Shinya Tsukamoto, Jap., 1995)

Topkapi (Jules Dassin, US, 1964)

Touchez pas au Grisbi (*Grisbi*) Jacques Becker, Fr./It., 1945)

Touch of Evil (Orson Welles, US, 1958)

True Romance (Tony Scott, US, 1993)

The Two Mrs. Carrolls (Peter Godfrey, US, 1947)

2001: A Space Odyssey (Stanley Kubrick, UK/US, 1968)

Undercurrent (Vincente Minnelli, US, 1946)

Underworld (Josef von Sternberg, US, 1927)

Underworld U.S.A. (Samuel Fuller, US, 1961)

The Usual Suspects (Bryan Singer, US/Ger., 1995)

U Turn (Oliver Stone, Fr./US, 1997)

Vertigo (Alfred Hitchcock, US, 1958)

Very Bad Things (Peter Berg, US, 1998)

De Vierde man (*The Fourth Man*) (Paul Verhoeven, Neth., 1983)

Vital (Shinya Tsukamoto, Jap., 2004)

Vivement dimanche (*Confidentially Yours*) (François Truffaut, Fr., 1983)

Von morgens bis mitternachts (*From Morn to Midnight*) (Karl Heinz Martin, Ger., 1920)

Das Wachsfigurenkabinett (*Waxworks*) (Paul Leni, Ger., 1924)

The War of the Roses (Danny DeVito, US, 1989)
The Web (Michael Gordon, US, 1947)
Weekend (Jean-Luc Godard, Fr., 1967)
Where the Sidewalk Ends (Otto Preminger, 1950)
While the City Sleeps (Fritz Lang, US, 1956)
White Heat (Raoul Walsh, US, 1949)
Wild at Heart (David Lynch, US, 1990)
Winchester '73 (Anthony Mann, US, 1950)
The Window (Ted Tetzlaff, US, 1949)
The Woman in Green (Roy William Neill, US, 1945)
The Woman in the Window (Fritz Lang, US, 1945)
The Wrong Man (Alfred Hitchcock, US, 1957)
Yojimbo (Akira Kurosawa, Jap., 1961)
You Only Live Once (Fritz Lang, US, 1937)

BIBLIOGRAPHY

Adorno, Theodor W. and Max Horkheimer (1997) [1944] *Dialectic of Enlightenment*. Translated by John Cumming. London: Verso.

Althusser, Louis (1971) [1969] 'Ideology and Ideological State Apparatuses (Notes Towards an Investigation)', in *Lenin and Philosophy and Other Essays*. Translated by Ben Brewster. London: NLB, 121–73.

Altman, Rick (1999) *Film/Genre*. London: British Film Institute.

Andrew, Dudley (1995) *Mists of Regret: Culture and Sensibility in Classic French Film*. Princeton: Princeton University Press.

Barefoot, Guy (2001) *Gaslight Melodrama: From Victorian London to 1940s Hollywood*. New York: Continuum.

Barlow, John D. (1982) *German Expressionist Cinema*. Boston: Twayne.

Bernstein, Matthew and Gaylyn Studlar (eds) (1997) *Visions of the East: Orientalism in Film*. London: I. B. Tauris.

Bogdanovich, Peter (1997) *Who the Devil Made It*. New York: Ballantine.

Boler, Jay and Richard Grusin (1999) *Remediation: Understanding New Media*. Cambridge, MA: MIT Press.

Borde, Raymonde and Etienne Chaumeton (2002) [1955] *A Panorama of American Film Noir, 1941–1953*. Translated by Paul Hammond. San Francisco: City Lights Books.

Bordwell, David (1985) *Narration in the Fiction Film*. London: Methuen.

Bordwell, David, Janet Staiger and Kristin Thompson (1988) *The Classical Hollywood Cinema: Film Style and Mode of Production to 1960*. London: Routledge.

Bottomore, Tom, Laurence Harris, V. G. Kiernan and Ralph Miliband (eds)

(1991) *A Dictionary of Marxist Thought* (second edition). Oxford: Blackwell.

Bould, Mark (2002) 'The Dreadful Credibility of Absurd Things: A Tendency in Fantasy Theory', *Historical Materialism: Research in Critical Marxist Theory*, 10, 4, 51–88.

____ (2003) 'Apocalypse Here and Now: Making Sense of *The Texas Chain Saw Massacre*', in Gary D. Rhodes (ed.) (2003) *Horror at the Drive-In: Essays in Popular Americana*. Jefferson: McFarland, 97–112.

Bradbury, Malcolm and James McFarlane (eds) (1976) *Modernism, 1890–1930*. London: Penguin.

Britton, Andrew (1992) '*Detour*', in Ian Cameron (ed.) *The Movie Book of Film Noir*. London: Studio Vista, 174–83.

Bukatman, Scott (1993) *Terminal Identity: The Virtual Subject in Postmodern Science Fiction*. Durham: Duke University Press.

Buss, Robin (1994) *French Film Noir*. New York: Marion Boyars.

Cain, James M. (2002) *Double Indemnity*. London: Orion.

Cameron, Ian (ed.) (1992) *The Movie Book of Film Noir*. London: Studio Vista.

Chabrol, Claude (1985) [1955] 'Evolution of the Thriller', translated by Liz Heron, in Jim Hillier (ed.) *Cahiers du Cinéma. The 1950s: Neo-Realism, Hollywood, New Wave*. Cambridge: Harvard University Press, 158–64.

Chandler, Raymond (1980) 'Introduction', to *Pearls Are a Nuisance. The Chandler Collection, vol. III*, London: Picador, 9–12.

Chartier, Jean-Pierre (1996) [1946] 'The Americans Are Making Dark Films Too', translated by R. Barton Palmer, in R. Barton Palmer (ed.) *Perspectives on Film Noir*. New York: G. K. Hall, 25–7.

Coates, Paul (1991) *The Gorgon's Gaze: German Cinema, Expressionism, and the Image of Horror*. Cambridge: Cambridge University Press.

Collins, Chik (2000) 'Vygotsky on Language and Social Consciousness: Underpinning the Use of Voloshinov in the Study of Popular Protest', *Historical Materialism: Research in Critical Marxist Theory*, 7, 41–69.

Copjec, Joan (ed.) (1993) *Shades of Noir: A Reader*. London: Verso.

Corber, Robert J. (1997) *Homosexuality in Cold War America: Resistance and the Crisis of Masculinity*. Durham: Duke University Press.

Crisp, Colin (1993) *The Classic French Cinema: 1930–1960*. Bloomington: Indiana University Press.

Daly, Carroll John (1985) [1923] 'Three Gun Terry', in William F. Nolan (ed.)

Black Mask Boys: Masters in the Hard-Boiled School of Detective Fiction. New York: Mysterious Press, 43–72.

Damico, James (1996) [1978] 'Film Noir: A Modest Proposal', in R. Barton Palmer (ed.) *Perspectives on Film Noir.* New York: G. K. Hall, 129–40.

Davis, Mike (1986) *Prisoners of the American Dream: Politics and Economy in the History of the U.S. Working Class.* London: Verso.

Diawara, Manthia (1993) 'Noir by Noirs: Towards a New Realism in Black Cinema', in Joan Copjec (ed.) *Shades of Noir: A Reader.* London: Verso, 261–78.

Dimendberg, Edward (2004) *Film Noir and the Spaces of Modernity.* Cambridge: Harvard University Press.

Dmytryk, Edward (1996) *Odd Man Out: A Memoir of the Hollywood Ten.* Carbondale and Edwardsville: Southern Illinois University Press.

Duncan, Paul (2003) *The Pocket Essential Film Noir* (revised edition). Harpenden: Pocket Essentials.

Durgnat, Raymond (1996) [1970] 'Paint It Black: The Family Tree of the *Film Noir*', in R. Barton Palmer (ed.) *Perspectives on Film Noir.* New York: G. K. Hall, 83–98.

Duvillars, Pierre (1996) [1951] 'She Kisses Him So He'll Kill', (translated by R. Barton Palmer) in R. Barton Palmer (ed.) *Perspectives on Film Noir.* New York: G. K. Hall, 30–2.

Earman, John (1986) *A Primer on Determinism.* Dordrecht: D. Reidel.

Eisner, Lotte (1977) [1952] *The Haunted Screen: Expressionism in the German Cinema and the Influence of Max Reinhardt.* Translated by Roger Greaves. Berkeley: University of California Press.

Elsaesser, Thomas (2000) *Weimar Cinema and After: Germany's Historical Imaginary.* London: Routledge.

Elsaesser, Thomas with Adam Barker (eds) (1990) *Early Cinema: Space, Frame, Narrative.* London: British Film Institute.

Forter, Greg (2000) *Murdering Masculinities: Fantasies of Gender and Violence in the American Crime Novel.* New York: New York University Press.

Frank, Nino (1996) [1946] 'The Crime Adventure Story: A New Kind of Detective Film', translated by R. Barton Palmer, in R. Barton Palmer (ed.) *Perspectives on Film Noir.* New York: G. K. Hall, 21–4.

Fukuyama, Francis (1992) *The End of History and the Last Man.* London: Penguin.

Gledhill, Christine (1998a) [1978] 'Klute 1: A Contemporary Film Noir and Feminist Criticism', in E. Ann Kaplan (ed.) Women in Film Noir (second edition). London: British Film Institute, 20–34.

_____ (1998b) [1978] 'Klute 2: Feminism and Klute', in E. Ann Kaplan (ed.) Women in Film Noir (second edition). London: British Film Institute, 99–114.

Gramsci, Antonio (1998) Selections from the Prison Notebooks of Antonio Gramsci, edited and translated by Quintin Hoare and Geoffrey Nowell Smith. London: Lawrence and Wishart.

Gunning, Tom (2000) The Films of Fritz Lang: Allegories of Vision and Modernity. London: British Film Institute.

Hall, Nina (ed.) (1992) The New Scientist Guide to Chaos. London: Penguin.

Hammett, Dashiell (1985) [1923] 'Bodies Piled Up', in William F. Nolan (ed.) Black Mask Boys: Masters in the Hard-Boiled School of Detective Fiction. New York: Mysterious Press, 80–91.

Harvey, Sylvia (1998) 'Woman's Place: The Absent Family of Film Noir', in E. Ann Kaplan (ed.) Women in Film Noir (second edition). London: British Film Institute, 35–46.

Hayles, N. Katherine (1990) Chaos Bound: Orderly Disorder in Contemporary Literature and Science. Ithaca: Cornell University Press.

_____ (ed.) (1991) Chaos and Order: Complex Dynamics in Literature and Science. Chicago: University of Chicago Press.

Hayward, Susan (1993) French National Cinema. London: Routledge.

Held, David (1991) 'Frankfurt School', in Tom Bottomore, Laurence Harris, V. G. Kiernan and Ralph Miliband (eds) A Dictionary of Marxist Thought (second edition). Oxford: Blackwell. 208–13.

Herf, Jeffrey (1984) Reactionary Modernism: Technology, Culture and Politics in Weimar and the Third Reich. Cambridge: Cambridge University Press.

Higham, Charles and Joel Greenberg (1970) [1968] Hollywood in the Forties. New York: Coronet.

Hillier, Jim (ed.) (1985) Cahiers du Cinéma. The 1950s: Neo-Realism, Hollywood, New Wave. Cambridge: Harvard University Press.

Hirsch, Foster (1999) Detours and Lost Highways: A Map of Neo-Noir. New York: Limelight.

Hoefer, Carl (2003) 'Causal Determinism', in The Stanford Encyclopedia of Philosophy at http://plato.stanford.edu/entries/determinism-causal

Iampolski, Mikhail (1998) *The Memory of Tiresias: Intertextuality and Film*, translated by Harsha Ram. Berkeley: University of California Press.

Jacobowitz, Florence (1992) [1988] 'The Man's Melodrama: *The Woman in the Window* & *Scarlet Street*' in Ian Cameron (ed.) *The Movie Book of Film Noir*. London: Studio Vista, 152–64.

Jacobs, Lea (1991) *The Wages of Sin: Censorship and the Fallen Woman Film, 1928–1942*. Madison: University of Wisconsin Press.

Jacobs, Lewis (ed.) (1977) *The Compound Cinema: The Film Writings of Harry Alan Potamkin*. New York: Teachers College Press.

James, C. L. R. (1993) *American Civilization*, edited and introduced by Anna Grimshaw and Keith Hart. Oxford: Blackwell.

Jameson, Fredric (1991) *Postmodernism, or, The Cultural Logic of Late Capitalism*. London: Verso.

Jeter, K. W. (1995) *Blade Runner 2: The Edge of Human*. London: Orion.

Kaes, Anton (2001) *M* (revised edition). London: British Film Institute.

Kaes, Anton, Martin Jay and Edward Dimendberg (eds) (1994) *The Weimar Republic Sourcebook*. Berkeley: California University Press.

Kaplan, E. Ann (ed.) (1998a) *Women in Film Noir* (second edition). London: British Film Institute.

_____ (1998b) 'The "Dark Continent" of Film Noir: Race, Displacement and Metaphor in Tourneur's *Cat People* (1942) and Welles' *The Lady from Shanghai* (1948)', in E. Ann Kaplan (ed.) *Women in Film Noir* (second edition). London: British Film Institute, 183–201.

Kawin, Bruce (1978) *Mindscreen: Bergman, Godard, and First-Person Film*. Princeton: Princeton University Press.

Kerr, Paul (1996) [1979] 'Out of What Past? Notes on the B *film noir*', in Alain Silver and James Ursini (eds) *Film Noir Reader*. New York: Limelight, 107–27.

Kracauer, Siegfried (1974) [1947] *From Caligari to Hitler: A Psychological History of German Film*. Princeton: Princeton University Press.

Krutnik, Frank (1991) *In a Lonely Street: Film Noir, Genre, Masculinity*. London: Routledge.

Laqueur, Walter (1974) *Weimar – A Cultural History*. London: Weidenfeld and Nicolson.

Lev, Peter (2003) *Transforming the Screen, 1950–1959*. New York: Scribner's.

Madden, David (ed.) (1968) *Tough Guy Writers of the Thirties*. Carbondale:

Southern Illinois University Press.

Maltby, Richard (2003) *Hollywood Cinema* (second edition). Oxford: Blackwell.

Marling, William (1995) *The American Roman Noir: Hammett, Cain, and Chandler*. Athens: University of Georgia Press.

Martin, Richard (1997) *Mean Streets and Raging Bulls: The Legacy of Film Noir in Contemporary American Cinema*. Lanham: Scarecrow.

McCann, Sean (2000) *Gumshoe America: Hard-Boiled Crime Fiction and the Rise and Fall of New Deal Liberalism*. Durham: Duke University Press.

McNally, David (1995) 'Language, History and Class Struggle', *Monthly Review*, 47, 3, 13–30.

____ (2001) *Bodies of Meaning: Studies on Language, Labor, and Liberation*. Albany: State University of New York Press.

Monaco, Paul (1976) *Cinema & Society: France and Germany During the Twenties*. New York: Elsevier.

Morgan, Janice (1997) 'In the Labyrinth: Masculine Subjectivity, Expatriation and Colonialism in *Pépé le Moko*', in Matthew Bernstein and Gaylyn Studlar (eds) *Visions of the East: Orientalism in Film*. London: I. B. Tauris, 253–68.

Moylan, Tom (1986) *Demand the Impossible: Science Fiction and the Utopian Imagination*. London: Methuen.

Mulvey, Laura (1989) [1975] 'Visual Pleasure and Narrative Cinema', in *Visual and Other Pleasures*. Basingstoke: Macmillan, 14–26.

Munby, Jonathan (1999) *Public Enemies, Public Heroes: Screening the Gangster from Little Caesar to Touch of Evil*. Chicago: University of Chicago Press.

Musser, Charles (1990) [1984] 'The Travel Genre in 1903–1904: Moving Towards Fictional Narrative', in Thomas Elsaesser with Adam Barker (eds) *Early Cinema: Space, Frame, Narrative*. London: British Film Institute, 123–32.

Naremore, James (1998) *More than Night: Film Noir in its Contexts*. Berkeley: University of California Press.

Neale, Steve (2000) *Genre and Hollywood*. London: Routledge.

____ (ed.) (2002) *Genre and Contemporary Hollywood*. London: British Film Institute.

Newman, Kim (1989) *The Night Mayor*. London: Simon & Schuster.

Nolan, William F. (1985) *Black Mask Boys: Masters in the Hard-Boiled School of Detective Fiction*. New York: Mysterious Press.

O'Brien, Charles (1996) 'Film Noir in France: Before the Liberation', *Iris*, 21, 7–20.

O'Brien, Geoffrey (1997) *Hardboiled America: Lurid Paperbacks and the Masters of Noir* (expanded edition). New York: Da Capo Press.

O'Connell, Jack (ed.) (2002) *Dark Alleys of Noir. Paradoxa*, 16.

O'Shaughnessy, Martin (1996) *'Pépé le Moko*, or the Impossibility of Being French in the 1930s', *French Cultural Studies*, 7, 247–58.

Oliver, Kelly and Benigno Trigo (2003) *Noir Anxiety*. Minneapolis: University of Minnesota Press.

Palmer, R. Barton (ed.) (1996) *Perspectives on Film Noir*. New York: G. K. Hall.

Petrie, Graham (1985) *Hollywood Destinies: European Directors in America 1922–1931*. London: Routledge & Kegan Paul.

Petro, Patrice (1989) *Joyless Streets: Women and Melodramatic Representation in Weimar Germany*. Princeton: Princeton University Press.

Place, J. A. and L. S. Peterson (1996) [1974], 'Some Visual Motifs of *Film Noir*', in Alain Silver and James Ursini (eds) *Film Noir Reader*. New York: Limelight, 64–75.

Porfirio, Robert (1999) 'Dark Jazz: Music in the Film Noir' in Alain Silver and James Ursini (eds) *Film Noir Reader 2*. New York: Limelight, 177–87.

_____ (2001) 'Miklós Rózsa (1907–1995)', in Robert Porfirio, Alain Silver and James Ursini (eds) *Film Noir Reader 3: Interviews with Filmmakers of the Classic Noir Period*. New York: Limelight, 163–76.

Porfirio, Robert, Alain Silver and James Ursini (eds) (2001) *Film Noir Reader 3: Interviews with Filmmakers of the Classic Noir Period*. New York: Limelight.

Potamkin, Harry (1977) [1930] 'The Racketeer Paramount', in Lewis Jacobs (ed.) *The Compound Cinema: The Film Writings of Harry Alan Potamkin*. New York: Teachers College Press, 477–9.

Prawer, S. S. (2002) *The Blue Angel (Der Blaue Engel)*. London: British Film Institute.

Prigogine, Ilya and Isabelle Stengers (1985) *Order Out of Chaos: Man's New Dialogue with Nature*. London: Flamingo.

Pye, Douglas (1992) 'Film Noir and Suppressive Narrative: *Beyond a Reasonable Doubt*', in Ian Cameron (ed.) *The Movie Book of Film Noir*. London: Studio Vista, 98–109.

Rabinowitz, Paula (2002) *Black & White & Noir: America's Pulp Modernism*. New York: Columbia University Press.

Reid, David and Jayne L. Walker (1993) 'Strange Pursuit: Cornell Woolrich and the Abandoned City of the Forties', in Joan Copjec (ed.) *Shades of Noir: A Reader*. London: Verso, 57–96.

Rey, Henri-François (1996) [1948] 'Hollywood Makes Myths like Ford Makes Cars (last installment): Demonstration by the Absurd: Films Noirs', Translated by R. Barton Palmer, in R. Barton Palmer (ed) *Perspectives on Film Noir*. New York: G. K. Hall, 28–9.

Rhodes, Gary D. (2003) *Horror at the Drive-In: Essays in Popular Americana*. Jefferson: McFarland.

Richardson, Carl (1992) *Autopsy: An Element of Realism in Film Noir*. Metuchen: Scarecrow Press.

Sandler, Kevin S. (2002) 'Movie Ratings as Genre: The Incontestable R', in Steve Neale (ed.) *Genre and Contemporary Hollywood*. London: British Film Institute, 201–17.

Schatz, Thomas (1997) *Boom and Bust: American Cinema in the 1940s*. Berkeley: University of California Press.

Schrader, Paul (1996) [1972] 'Notes on Film Noir', in R. Barton Palmer (ed.) *Perspectives on Film Noir*. New York: G. K. Hall, 99–109.

Shearer, Lloyd (1999) [1945] 'Crime Certainly Pays on the Screen', in Alain Silver and James Ursini (eds) *Film Noir Reader 2*. New York: Limelight, 9–13.

Sheppard, Richard (1976) 'German Expressionism', in Malcolm Bradbury and James McFarlane (eds) *Modernism, 1890–1930*. London: Penguin, 274–91.

Silver, Alain and James Ursini (eds) (1996) *Film Noir Reader*. New York: Limelight.

____ (eds) (1999) *Film Noir Reader 2*. New York: Limelight.

Silver, Alain and Elizabeth Ward (eds) (1992) *Film Noir: An Encyclopedic Reference to the American Style* (3rd edition). New York: Overlook Press.

Skal, David J. (1993) *The Monster Show: A Cultural History of Horror*. London: Plexus.

Sloterdijk, Peter (1988) *Critique of Cynical Reason*. Translated by Michael Eldred. London: Verso.

Spicer, Andrew (2002) *Film Noir*. Harlow: Pearson.

Stewart, Garrett (1999) *Between Film and Screen: Modernism's Photo*

Synthesis. Chicago: University of Chicago Press.

Strebel, Elizabeth Grottle (1980) *French Social Cinema of the Nineteen-Thirties: A Cinematic Expression of Popular Front Consciousness*. New York: Arno.

Swift, Jonathan (1963) [1726] *Gulliver's Travels*. London: Oxford University Press.

Taylor, John Russell (1983) *Strangers in Paradise: The Hollywood Émigrés, 1933–1950*. London: Faber and Faber.

Telotte, J. P. (1989) *Voices in the Dark: The Narrative Patterns of Film Noir*. Urbana and Champaign: University of Illinois Press.

Theweleit, Klaus (1987) *Male Fantasies, vol. I: Women Floods Bodies History*. Translated by Stephen Conway, Erica Carter and Chris Turner. Minneapolis: University of Minnesota Press.

_____ (1989) *Male Fantasies, vol. II: Psychoanalyzing the White Terror*. Translated by Chris Turner, Erica Carter and Stephen Conway. Minneapolis: University of Minnesota Press.

Thomas, Deborah (1992) [1988] 'How Hollywood Deals with the Deviant Male', in Ian Cameron (ed.) *The Movie Book of Film Noir*. London: Studio Vista, 59–70.

Thompson, John B. (1990) *Ideology and Modern Culture: Critical Social Theory in the Era of Mass Communication*. Cambridge: Polity Press.

Thomson, David (1997) *The Big Sleep*. London: British Film Institute.

Vernet, Marc (1993) '*Film Noir* on the Edge of Doom', in Joan Copjec (ed.) *Shades of Noir: A Reader*. London: Verso, 1–31.

Vincendeau, Ginette and Keith Reader (eds) (1986) *La Vie est à nous: French Cinema of the Popular Front, 1935–1938*. London: British Film Institute.

Vincendeau, Ginette (1998) *Pépé le Moko*. London: British Film Institute.

Wager, Jans B. (1999) *Dangerous Dames: Women and Representation in the Weimar Street Film and Film Noir*. Athens: Ohio University Press.

Walker, Michael (1992a) 'Film Noir: Introduction', in Ian Cameron (ed.) *The Movie Book of Film Noir*. London: Studio Vista, 8–38.

_____ (1992b) 'Robert Siodmak' in Ian Cameron (ed.) *The Movie Book of Film Noir*. London: Studio Vista, 110–51.

_____ (1992c) 'While the City Sleeps', *cineACTION*, 29, 56–69.

Wayne, Mike (2003) *Marxism and Media Studies: Key Concepts and Contemporary Trends*. London. Pluto.

Willeford, Charles (2000) *The Shark-Infested Custard*. Edinburgh: Canongate.

Williams, Linda Ruth (2004) 'No Sex Please We're American', *Sight and Sound*, 14, 1, 18–20.

Wright, Will (1977) *Sixguns and Society: A Structural Study of the Western*. Berkeley: University of California Press.

INDEX OF NAMES

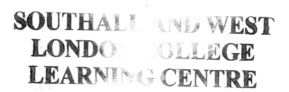